D1784683

To all Weegies.

FM

Editor: Nick Pierce
Artist: David Lyttleton
Additional artwork: Shutterstock

Published in Great Britain in MMXX by
Book House, an imprint of
The Salariya Book Company Ltd
25 Marlborough Place, Brighton BN1 1UB
www.salariya.com

ISBN: 978-1-912904-67-9

1 3 5 7 9 8 6 4 2

A CIP catalogue record for this book is available
from the British Library.

Printed and bound in China.
Printed on paper from sustainable sources.

Visit
www.salariya.com
for our online catalogue and
free fun stuff.

Glasgow

A Very

Peculiar History®

'Let Glasgow Flourish!'

Glasgow City Council motto

Glasgow

A Very Peculiar History®

Written by
Fiona Macdonald

Created and designed by
David Salariya

BOOK HOUSE
a SALARIYA imprint

'
I'll sing a song of Glasgow town...

First line of a poem by the
Glasgow-based pioneer feminist
poet, Marion Bernstein
(1846–1906)
'

Contents

'If the booze
doesn't get you, the
knife will.'

The Sun *newspaper, 2009*

STEREOTYPES, SUPERLATIVES, SURPRISES

Rough, dirty, drunken, quarrelsome, violent, unhealthy, economically depressed, culturally deprived, and speaking an incomprehensible dialect. Keelies! Weegies! Glaswegians! How we love to look down on them and their scruffy, sectarian, said-to-be-sordid city. We're told it's a Scottish slum. A no-go area. Uncouth, uncivilised, ugly in body and soul, especially when compared with its rival: refined, intellectual and oh-so-elegant Edinburgh. Yes? Well – no, actually.

Aye, right?

Over the years, more ill-informed and ill-mannered rubbish has been written about Glasgow and its inhabitants than anywhere else in the UK. If the stereotypes are to be believed, then Glasgow is a post-industrial wasteland, full of pollution, dereliction and grim tower blocks. Where depressed unemployed men – and fierce unemployable women – lurk and fight in mean streets or sordid drinking dens, and malnourished children face a hopeless future, doomed to die at an earlier age than anywhere else in Britain. An urban desert where fresh fruit and vegetables are unknown, and inhabitants live on greasy fish suppers or burnt rolls (see the box below), washed down with rust-coloured Irn-Bru or ironically named Buckfast 'Tonic' Wine. A city where no one wants to live, and even fewer wish to visit. A stagnant, redundant backwater with no redeeming features. A pit. A dump. A place to be avoided at all costs.

Nae mistake!

Well-fired rolls, with the upper crust blackened, have been sold in Glasgow and south-west Scotland for decades. So have their very close cousins, crispy-coated 'morning rolls', dusted with pale yellow coarse rice flour. Traditionally, well-fired rolls were eaten with square sausage or soup; they were also sought after as a cure for hangovers.

In 2018, hungry consumers of well-fired rolls, in Glasgow, Dundee* and many other Scottish cities, were startled to learn that their breakfast favourites were in danger of being banned. New health guidelines from the European Union warned that well-fired foods might cause cancer.

* Dundee Evening Telegraph, *12th April 2018*

Glasgow born – world famous!

Glasgow has been the birthplace of high achievers in many walks of life. Few world-famous Glaswegians still live or work in the city, but – who knows? – it might still give them extra edge and spark and energy. They include:

Lulu (singer, actor), Peter Capaldi (actor), Sir Alex Ferguson (football manager), Frankie Boyle (comedian), Sir Kenny Dalglish (footballer), Lorraine Kelly (TV presenter), Robert Carlyle (actor), Mark Knopfler (musician), Baroness Michelle Mone (ladies' underwear entrepreneur)

The Big Yin

Someone missing from that list? Yes, indeed. Sir William 'Billy' Connolly, CBE. After an abused childhood in a poor, overcrowded Glasgow tenement flat (now demolished), Connolly worked as a welder in Glasgow shipyards (now closed) and then as a folk-singer before winning world-wide fame as an original and outspoken comedian and as a movie actor. He lives mostly in the USA, but for several years also had an estate in the Scottish Highlands.

You're welcome!

But… wait a minute! If all these awful reports about Glasgow are true, then how do we explain the fact that it's been voted* one of the world's ten best cities to visit? In fact, it actually topped the same poll for both 'friendliness' and 'affordability', and won special praise for its 'dynamic' music, entertainment and food, plus the 'daft wit and gregariousness' of the locals. Visiting a city is not the same as living there, of course, but clearly, life in Glasgow is not as bad as it has sometimes been painted. Otherwise, why do 92% of Glaswegians reckon that their neighbourhood is a good place to stay?** Or 85% of Glasgow residents feel proud of their city?

If we look more closely, then many, many more positive facts and figures emerge from behind the smokescreen of tired stereotypes. Glasgow is Scotland's largest city, with a growing population. The wider Glasgow City Region is home to one-third of Scotland's people. Glasgow birth rates now exceed the

* *In a 2019 survey by Time Out.*
** *Scots for 'permanently reside'.*

death rates, and, for over 200 years, the city has welcomed migrants from many lands. Since 2011, Glasgow has been Scotland's most ethnically diverse community, with 12 per cent of its population not born in the UK. In 2016, it decisively voted 'remain' (by 66.6%) in the EU referendum.

When it comes to wealth creation, Glasgow ranks fourth in the UK, after London, Manchester and Birmingham.* Glasgow's enterprise, measured by the number of business start-ups in Scotland, is second only to oil-rich Aberdeen. And it's not all slums; three of its residential streets are listed among Scotland's top twenty most expensive addresses. Glasgow unemployment, although higher than the Scottish or UK average, is falling, with over two-thirds of Glaswegians of working age having a job. Hospitality and retail are big employers, together with finance, government and digital communications; in 2019 Glasgow was ranked the second most important 'Tech Cluster' city outside the London area. Glasgow's also one of the UK's most popular

* https://www.citymetric.com/business/where-are-britains-biggest-city-economies-2946

tourist destinations, and prides itself on being the best place in Scotland for shopping. It has very good public transport, including the world's only totally underground subway system – the famous 'Clockwork Orange'.

Glasgow boasts a year-round programme of world-class festivals and sporting events, has Europe's largest civic arts collection, and more green space per head of the population than any other European city – an amazing 90 public parks and gardens. It has some of Scotland's – no, the world's – finest 18th- and 19th- century architecture. It is home to 41% of Scotland's actors, dancers and broadcasters, 38% of its musicians and 29% of its artists and graphic designers.[*] It has a quite wonderful – if sadly accident prone – Art School. In 2016–2017, Glasgow's recorded crime rate (714 per 10,000 of the population) was considerably lower than London's. And, for what it's worth, in 2019 Glasgow was voted the 12th 'most hipster place in the UK'[**].

[*] https://www.understandingglasgow.com/indicators/cultural_vitality/overview
[**] 'Hipster heaven is found in Glasgow' by Marc Horne, The Times website, 7th January 2019

'Admit it: Glasgow has ruined you for life with its stunning parks, fantastic festivals and great food. You'll never love another city again.'

Hilary Mitchell, Buzzfeed, November 2014

Education, education...

The University of Glasgow – the fourth-oldest in the English-speaking world, and one of five in the city – has recently been ranked among the global top 100. One-third of all adults in Glasgow have a degree. And almost nine out of every ten Glasgow citizens took part in some sort of 'cultural activity' in 2016. The most popular were reading, creative computing and crafts, but plenty of Glaswegians also visited cinemas (61%), museums (46%), live music events (38%), libraries (34%) and theatres (30%).* They're certainly a lively-minded lot!

* *https://www.understandingglasgow.com/indicators/cultural_vitality/overview*

...and heritage, and culture...

Looking back a bit, Glasgow can boast of a patron saint with two names, one of Scotland's few surviving medieval buildings (the Cathedral), and the tomb of romantic lovers' favourite, St Valentine – well, at least part of him (see page 57). It is home to the world's oldest surviving music-hall and tallest cinema. It has the only building, anywhere, that can rotate 360 degrees on its own axis into the prevailing wind. That's the unhappily nicknamed 'White Elephant', officially the Glasgow Tower, completed in 2001. No, I don't know what it's for, either. It's immensely impressive, however – and ever so slightly scary. It sways in the wind and, to be allowed inside, visitors must declare that they'd be capable of descending all 523 steps down from the top, if the lifts were to fail. Glasgow also has one of Europe's largest public libraries (the Mitchell Library), Europe's longest bar and a stunning waterfront building by fashionable and revolutionary architect Dame Zaha Hadid.

Made in Glasgow

Glasgow also has an awful lot of world 'firsts' to its name – including the world's first ocean-going steamship and the world's first hospital X-ray department. Waterproof clothing, refrigerators and ATM (cash-dispensing) machines were invented there. It was also the first UK city to ban indoor public smoking and to train the first UK female professional lawyer. Glasgow was the site of the first-ever official international football match (and between women's teams, too), home to Scotland's first public museum (opened 1807), received the world's first broadcast television signal (1926, all the way from London) – and much, much more. You can read about many futher great Glasgow achievements later in this book.

Rich and poor

Sadly, deprivation and disadvantage still exist in Glasgow, though they tend to be concentrated in pockets, among the 25% of the Glasgow households where no one is listed as being economically active. Government statistics also reveal vast differences in child poverty across the city, from a staggering 59% in one neighbourhood to a tiny 5% in another. Recent research tells of another worrying trend: the proportion of people in work but living in poverty has been rising; in 2015–2016, 64% of working-age adults in poverty lived in a household where at least one person had a job. In this respect, Glasgow is similar to – and slightly worse – than the rest of Scotland.

In spite of inequality, poverty and deprivation, Glasgow is, as the saying has it, 'no mean city'. Glasgow government slogans have also claimed that 'Glasgow Smiles Better' and 'People Make Glasgow'. Yes, it really is an exceptionally friendly place. And open-hearted, and with a strong sense of egalitarianism and individual pride.

Exceptionally outspoken, too...

Glasgow facts and figures

Latitude: 55.8609 N (north of Moscow!)
Longitude: 4.2514 W

Location: On the banks of the River Clyde, in the Central Belt of Scotland

Climate: Cool, wet, often overcast. Sometimes said to be the rainiest city in the UK, with an average 170 days of rainfall.

Hottest month: July, average high 19 °C
Coldest month: December, average low 1.7 °C
Sunniest month: May, average 180 hours
Wettest month: January, average 148 mm

Maximum high recorded: 31.9 °C (June 2018)
Minimum low recorded: −14.5 °C
(December 1982)

Area: 176 square km   (City)
        3,338 square km (City Region)

Population (2017): 621,020   (City)
                 1,817,870 (City Region)

Population density: 3,528 per sq km (City)
          540 per sq km (City Region)

Governing body: Glasgow City Council (City)

Atlantic
Ocean

N
W E
S

Scotland

•Aberdeen

•Dundee

North
Sea

Glasgow•
•Edinburgh

Central
Belt

Irish Sea

Wales

England

Cardiff•

London •

English
Channel

Neighbours, all you need is neighbours...

In the past, there has sometimes been a prickly relationship between the central city 'heart' of Glasgow and the surrounding outer districts, which felt that their identity and independence were threatened, if not swamped, by their larger, more powerful neighbour. To take just two examples, residents of the great ship-building community of Clydebank, to the west of Glasgow, were not at all pleased when it was said – as it usually was – that majestic ocean liners such as the Queen Mary were 'built in Glasgow'. And the tough working-class district of Govan, on the south bank of the Clyde, resolutely followed a different calendar from Glasgow city when it came to arranging factory days off and holidays.

Over the past 200 years, there have been a baffling number of changes to local government administrative structures. Glasgow city legal boundaries have advanced and then retreated. It all became rather confusing. Residents could wake up one morning to find that they were no longer officially 'Glaswegian' – or that overnight they had become Glasgow citizens.

Since 2014, Glasgow plus the surrounding area has been known as Glasgow City Region. It is administered by eight separate local authorities:

- Glasgow
- East Dunbartonshire
- West Dunbartonshire
- North Lanarkshire
- South Lanarkshire
- East Renfrewshire
- Renfrewshire
- Inverclyde

In 2014, representatives of them all agreed on an ambitious new investment plan – the £1.13 billion 'City Deal' – to develop the Glasgow City Region as a whole.

So, what – and where – do people mean when they say 'Glasgow'? It changes, at different times and in different contexts. The answer's not always easy!

Dear Green Place – or Boggy Hollow?

What's in a name? Well, in Glasgow's case, there's quite a bit to think about. Rather surprisingly, 'Glasgow' is not Scots. Experts say that it's probably made up of two words in the ancient Brittonic tongue* – a language closely related to Welsh. It was spoken in the kingdoms of south-west Scotland and north-west England before around AD 800.

The words are 'Glas' (meaning 'grey, green or blue') plus Cau (meaning 'basin or hollow'). Put them together and you get 'Glasgu'. That's how Glasgow appears in the first written record of the name, made around AD 1116.

If you have a positive outlook on the world, you can interpret 'green' to mean grassy, fertile and pleasant, and think of a 'hollow' as a safe, sheltered refuge. Put them together and add a link to St Kentigern (see page 53), who deliberately chose to settle where Glasgow now stands... the result? 'Dear Green Place', which is how many Glasgow leaders have liked to describe their city.

* Also known as Brythonic, Cumbric or British, and very closely linked to, or even overlapping with, the Pritenic language spoken by Pictish peoples elsewhere in Scotland.

If you take a less rosy view of life, then grey / blue / green is the colour of a slow-flowing stream, just like the River Clyde, and a hollow is a low place where water can collect. Put them together, and, well – it's a soggy, boggy picture.

Alternatively, if you prefer to venture (quite far) beyond the boundaries of accepted explanation, you might want to support the theory put forward by accountant, insurance broker and amateur archaeologist Ludovic MacLellan Mann in 1939.

Sometimes nicknamed 'Glasgow's Indiana Jones', Mann was a passionate pioneer of the study of ancient remains, with a genius for publicity. He made important observations and discoveries in and around Glasgow, though his interpretations of what he found have often been challenged, in the past as well as today.

For example, Mann argued that the 'Glas' in Glasgow's name came from a very ancient word that meant 'shining', and that 'Cu' was an old name for the moon goddess. Therefore, he said, 'Glasgow' meant 'shining light of the moon'. And he was convinced that a temple to the goddess once stood on the site of the Necropolis – Glasgow's famous Victorian cemetery.

'On the edge of the
known world.'

The Romans' view
of the land where
Glasgow now stands.

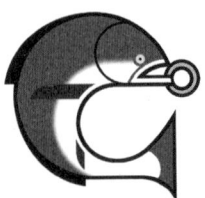

CHAPTER ONE

IN THE BEGINNING...

From fossils to fairy-folk, Glasgow's got the lot, hidden in its history. So where to start? It all depends on how far back we want to go, but the 'Fossil Grove' remains in a Glasgow public park date from way back before the dinosaurs. They are petrified trees from an extinct species (technically, rather like giant quillworts) about 320 million years old. They're from a time when Glasgow was tropically hot and even more rainy than it is today!

After that, about 3 million years ago, the glaciers came. As they froze and melted, froze and melted again, they changed the landscape, smoothing jagged mountains and carving out deep valleys. Glasgow is built in a wide, lowland basin covered by a 'swarm' of drumlins: little rounded hills created as glaciers crept across unstable ground. They look (or so it is said) 'like eggs in a basket'; many also have fertile, gravelly silt 'tails'. The Glasgow drumlins were formed when the most recent ice sheet covered most of western Scotland: a period known as the Loch Lomond Readvance, from around 12,900 BC to 11,500 BC.

To the south, the Glasgow basin is bordered by a long, low ridge; the highest point is Corse Hill (374 m), once the site of an early Christian meeting place, and guarded by a ruined medieval castle. To the north it's sheltered by the higher (578 m) Campsie Fells. These were formed by volcanic eruptions and are geologically very interesting; Campsie Glen is a RIGS*. For centuries – and still today – the fells have been well known as a source of pure drinking water.

*Regionally Important Geological and Geomorphological Site

'Sainsbury's Caledonian Still Water 4 x 2 l
Caledonian still Scottish water
Caledonian water from the Campsie Fells...'

*From Sainsbury's Supermarkets Ltd (GB) website,
2019*

Pedant alert! In fact, the Caledonii tribe, who
fought against the Romans, lived to the north
and east of the Campsie Fells. But it's a very
nice name for a brand.

A river runs through it...

Moving forwards several millennia, water
continued to play an important part in
Glasgow's development – especially Glasgow's
river:

'The Clyde, the Clyde, the beautiful Clyde,
The name of it thrills me and fills
me with pride...'

At the time that song was popular, in the 1940s and 1950s, the River Clyde as it ran through Glasgow was polluted, poisonous and lined on both banks with warehouses, docks and shipyards. Each to their own, of course. However, Ludovic Mann – we met him earlier, on page 23 – was not entirely misguided in linking Glasgow with a goddess. The River Clyde shares a name with Clota, a goddess (probably) worshipped by the Cumbric-speaking Damnonii tribe who lived in the Clyde valley. The tribe, and the name of the goddess, were recorded by Romans who occupied southern Scotland from around AD 79.

And the songwriters weren't really wrong, either. The Clyde is remarkable, in several ways. Scotland's second-longest river (after the Tay), it begins where two streams meet, high in the bare, bleak Lowther Hills of south Lanarkshire – an area known as 'God's Treasure House' because of the rich mineral deposits found there. (These include the gold used to make the Scottish royal crown, and lots of lead: poisonous but very useful.) It's also one of the coldest, snowiest regions of Scotland; one of the earliest curling clubs was founded there in 1777.

From the Lowther Hills, the Clyde runs north-west for 176 km until it reaches the Atlantic Ocean in a very wide (42 km) firth (the Scots name for estuary) – the largest and deepest enclosed area of sea water around the coast of the British Isles. Estuary waters are further sheltered by the Isle of Bute and the Kintyre peninsula, and warmed by the Gulf Stream.

Even before it reaches Glasgow, the Clyde flows through two further wonders. One is natural: a series of four spectacular waterfalls, or 'linns', in a steep wooded valley. The other is New Lanark, where Robert Owen (a leading supporter of progressive, co-operative ideals) took over water-powered cotton-spinning mills set up by his father-in-law, Glasgow industrialist David Dale, in 1786, and created a carefully planned 'model' community for over 2,500 workers.

Doon the watter*

The Clyde is wide – and far-reaching – but shallow and relatively safe as it flows through the low-lying area where Glasgow now stands. In prehistoric times, it was a highway into and out of Scotland's interior. Before farming developed in Scotland (between around 4000–3000 BC) and for many centuries after, much of Scotland was covered in dense birch and hazel scrub, which made overland travel very difficult indeed. Rivers were the ideal alternative, and allowed hunters or would-be farmer settlers to move inwards, from around the coasts. And rivers were probably full of fish and water-birds – a safer source of food than heading out to sea.

We don't have much prehistoric evidence of human habitation for the Glasgow region (it's been destroyed by later industrial building), but what we DO have is often waterlogged – for example, the soggy remains of a wooden

* *Down the Water/River: a 19th/20th century name for very popular boat trips on the Clyde, from Glasgow to the sea.*

dug-out canoe, maybe made around 5000 BC, from the River Clyde. There are also some stone and bone tools, dredged up from the river gravels, including, for example, a smooth, polished axe found in the saturated remains of a dug-out log boat. Its design and manufacture have been linked by some archaeologists to the migration of Stone-Age farmers to western Scotland from Brittany, around 4000 BC.

More Water – the Molendinar (say: Mul~en~DIE~nar) Burn

This is a stream that runs southwards from two little lochs to the north of what is now Glasgow and down into the Clyde. The name mean's 'Miller's Stream' – it refers to water mills located there in the Middle Ages. Three more little rivulets join it, closer to the Clyde. The Molendinar brings silt with it, making the River Clyde even shallower and narrower. Here is where the first Glasgow river crossing was almost certainly made – and where the city's first bridge was later built in medieval times.

Puzzle panel

Historians suggest that fishing and maybe fish-trading settlements grew up on both banks of the Clyde, as hunter-gatherers settled down and began farming. Over the centuries, away from the river, scattered farming hamlets developed across the whole Glasgow basin area. Not much evidence remains, but what does is interesting:

Today, Mount Vernon is an affluent commuter suburb in south Glasgow, about a kilometre north of the Clyde. But in the early Bronze Age (between around 2700 BC and 1400 BC) life there was very different. In 1928, workmen uncovered the following items in a sand quarry:

- a skull
- three pottery containers
- some little stone kists (burial boxes) – these contained the remains of (among others) an elderly man, a young woman and a teenager
- The old man was buried with a flint arrowhead. The young woman was buried with a flint knife, a white pebble and food-storage pot containing traces of oats and rye. The teenager had been covered by (or was wearing) a garment of soft moss, with a food-storage pot close by.

Cup and ring

Head westward from Mount Vernon, and there's another tantalising remnant of Glasgow's distant past: the giant (13 x 7 m) Cochno Stone, a huge slab of rock now in the middle of a 'scheme' (local authority housing estate) at Faifley, about 13 km from Glasgow city centre.

Well-known for centuries (the old Gaelic name for the site means 'field of the rock'), the Cochno stone is recognised today as 'the finest set of cup and ring marks in existence'.[*] It dates from around 3000 BC.

Cup and ring marks? What, who, why? Well, they look like little round hollows surrounded by grooved circles. They are found along the Atlantic seaboard of Europe, and inland from Scandinavia to Greece. They were clearly made by skilled craftworkers, who combined precise use of tools with artistic flair and (probably) some kind of belief system, and were able to devote time and energy to training and to their work while other community members hunted or grew food.

[*] K. Brophy, Scottish Archaeological Journal 40 (1), March 2018

However, no one is really certain what cup and ring marks mean or what their purpose was. It used to be thought that they might be a form of writing or even a system of measurement, but more recently it's been suggested that they are boundary markers, perhaps linked to land ownership. Or else that they were used to separate farmland from wild land used for hunting.

Even more mysteriously, the Cochno Stone is marked with two carved pairs of footprints – although each of the four footprints only has four toes... Are these peculiar prints some sign of ownership? Was standing in them perhaps part of a ritual? (This happened almost 3,000 years later, when early kings of Scotland were proclaimed at Dunadd, not that far away.) Or are the prints symbols – of what? – rather than pictorial records?

Rather sadly, since 1965, the Cochno Stone has had to be covered over, to protect it from vandalism.

The Picts woz here

We don't know the name of the tribe or community that created the marks on the Cochno Stone. They left no written records. The first-known words we have to link us to the people in Glasgow's past date from the time when another mysterious people, the Picts, lived in the Glasgow area, from around 1 BC to AD 800.

All kinds of weird theories have sprung up to describe the Picts, suggesting that they were Pygmies from Africa, for example, or lived in holes in the ground and only came out at night, like fairies, or believed themselves to be descendants of the fertility goddess, Brigid. Less romantically but more factually, the Picts were probably a confederation of Scottish tribes that fought against Roman and other invaders. They spoke Pritenic – a language closely related to Cumbric and Welsh and more distantly to Scottish Gaelic. They were fighters but also farmers, hunters, builders and highly skilled stone-workers. They had kings, and also Christian priests, monks and nuns after around AD 500.

A few Pictish names were recorded by Roman visitors to Scotland. Pictish people are mentioned by Northumbrian monk and scholar, the Venerable Bede (d. AD 735). And medieval copies of lists of Pictish kings still survive, dating back to around AD 300. Just as importantly, Pictish place names survive in many parts of Scotland, to tell us where the Picts lived, or were powerful.

As we saw on page 22, Glasgow's name comes from two Cumbric words that Pictish people would have known and understood. Other place names with Cumbric/Pictish origins* in Glasgow include:

- Barlanark (boar wood)
- Govan (small hill)
- Partick (little thicket)
- Possil (resting place).

* Information from: https://www.celticstudiescongress.org/index.php/home/ceiltisglaschu/celtic-placenames-glasgow/

A wall too far?

By the first century AD, the Romans had arrived in Scotland, though they did not stop off in what is now Glasgow as they marched northwards. (It's thought they forded the River Clyde at Dumbuck, where traces of a causeway have been discovered.) However, just 16 km west of Glasgow, in the village known today as Old Kilpatrick, Roman army commanders sited the western terminus of their furthest frontier: the Antonine Wall. Its purpose? To defend Roman-occupied territory against Pictish tribes from the north.

Although hardly the most challenging part of Scotland in which to live – this is not the Highlands – the Romans found the Antonine Wall very hard work to maintain, supply and defend. Building started in AD 142. Around seven thousand soldiers, sheltering on site in wooden huts or leather tents (fragments still survive, plus metal tent pegs), cut and piled up slabs of turf to create a barrier 3 metres high and 60 km long. On the Wall's northern side, they dug a ditch 5 metres deep, and used the earth from this ditch to create an outer ring-shaped defensive mound.

Roman soldier-labourers also built 17 (or maybe 19) forts where men defending the wall and their commanding officers could live in safety, and many smaller fortlets to shelter troops fighting in skirmishes or out on patrol. Some forts, like the one at Bearsden (now a suburb of Glasgow) had splendid bath-houses, drains and communal lavatories. A well-constructed military road ran close to the south side of the Wall, so that soldiers, supplies and building materials could get to it as quickly as possible, and messengers could carry dispatches from Roman army headquarters further south.

After all this careful planning, clever logistics and back-breaking effort, the Antonine Wall was left unguarded and unmaintained after around AD 158, when the emperor recalled troops to Rome. It was rebuilt and re-occupied from around AD 208. The wall was abandoned and all the forts demolished when the Romans sailed away from the British Isles in AD 411. But the wall survived and can still be visited – and admired – today.

Multi-cultural

The Roman army was led by Roman citizen officers, but recruited auxiliary legions from all over the conquered Roman Empire lands. Several divisions of soldiers stationed on the Antonine Wall came from North Africa, and pottery fragments of distinctive African design have been found at its forts.

Dead letters?

Rather sweetly, Google Maps maintains that the Antonine Wall has a postcode (G65 0SA). We all know that Roman soldiers at Vindolanda Fort on Hadrian's Wall, further south, liked writing home to Mum. But even so...

Going further?

In spite of Glasgow's many later achievements – including all its motorways (see page 174) – the Antonine Wall remains the biggest engineering project ever undertaken in the Glasgow region. But while building their wall, did the Romans – on or off-duty – ever visit the little Glasgow basin settlements beside the Clyde, or trade with the farmers and fishermen living there? Yes, probably.

Building walls is hard work, and Roman soldiers needed feeding. They also needed raw materials – especially timber and leather –

woollen clothes to keep the cold out and little luxuries such as dice made from bone or deer antler.

There were other, less peaceful contacts. In an attempt to show the local Picts who was boss, Roman soldiers put up stone-slab distance markers at intervals along the wall. They decorated these with lifelike carvings of savage wild beasts and slaughtered enemies, *pour encourager les autres*. Recent research has revealed that these were once brightly and bloodthirstily painted.

Let's end this chapter with another mysterious, just possibly prehistoric, Glasgow relic. It's an earthwork in Queen's Park – a beautiful 19th-century public open space in the south of the city. Known today as Camp Hill, this earthwork consists of a huge steep-sided mound surrounded by a circular ditch. On top of the mound, archaeologists have discovered traces of a wooden stockade and husks of grain. Roman pottery fragments have been found in the steep bank and medieval pottery at the bottom of the ditch.

Clearly this was a fort of some kind, but when was it built, and by whom? Perhaps during the Iron Age (c 700 BC–AD 500) by Pictish tribes, defending themselves from Roman (or other) invaders? Or by a posse of Roman soldiers, on their way to or from the nearby Antonine Wall? Or more probably, as the most recent archaeologists have suggested, by early medieval Scots copying Norman-French fashions to construct an early motte-and-bailey castle. Even if that is true, some Romans must have been there – and dropped pots – before later occupants arrived.

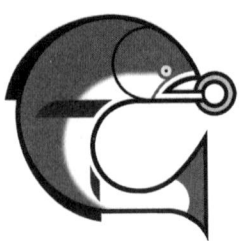

' There's the tree
that never grew,
There's the fish
that never swam,
There's the bird
that never flew,
There's the bell
that never rang. '

Traditional puzzle-rhyme
describing the miracles
of St Kentigern (aka St
Mungo). Read more on
page 56.

CHAPTER TWO

SAINTS AND SELLERS

You want saints? Glasgow's got several. And they played an important part in the development of the city. They lived at a time when Scotland was changing from a pre-Christian tribal society to a small cluster of kingdoms ruled by Christian monarchs – and being attacked by Viking raiders meanwhile. Yes, these are the so-called 'Dark Ages', and from around AD 400 to AD 1100 they are indeed pretty obscure when it comes to Glasgow's history.

Documents providing evidence of Dark Age life on the banks of the Clyde are few and far between, and early chroniclers, where most of our evidence comes from, were not shy of inventing exciting details when they were running short of facts. However, so far as we can tell, there was nothing out of the ordinary happening on the site where Glasgow now stands before the year AD 543. Fishermen went on fishing, farmers went on farming and boatbuilders crafted coracles from wood and leather. According to Greco-Roman geographer Ptolemy (d. AD 170), the Clyde basin was inhabited by members of the Cumbric/Brythonic-speaking Damnonii tribe, who had links to, and were sometimes attacked by, Gaelic speakers from Ireland and the far-west Scottish kingdom of Dalriada, and by Picts from further north.

From around AD 450, different tribes throughout Scotland slowly began to group together – or be grouped together by conquest – under the rule of local kings. Gradually, Scotland became divided into four main kingdoms, which stretched southwards beyond the present-day Scottish-English border.

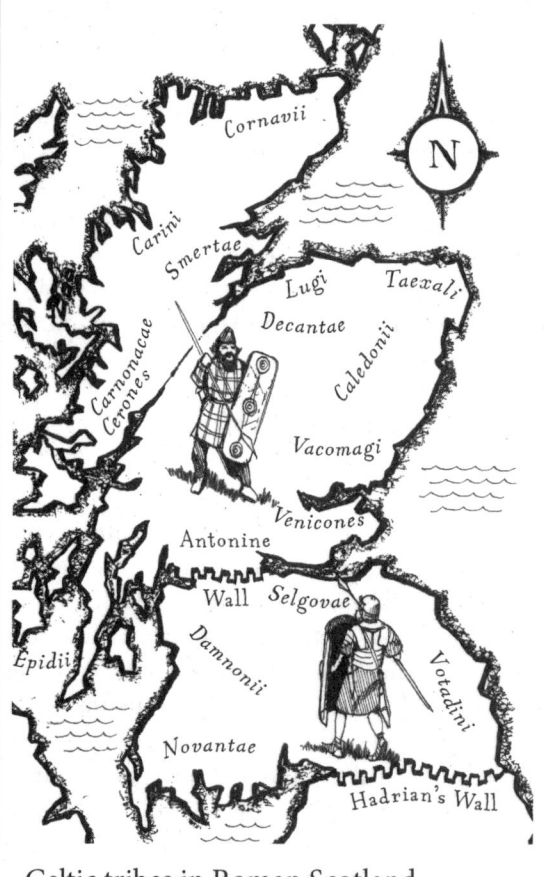

Celtic tribes in Roman Scotland

The site of Glasgow belonged to the kingdom of Alt Clut (the rock of the Clyde) also known as Strathclyde (the wide valley of the River Clyde). This was controlled by rulers based at the splendid natural fortress now known as Dumbarton Rock. Used as a stronghold since before Roman times, and for many centuries later – Mary Queen of Scots was sent there for safety – Dumbarton Rock was also said to have been visited by the legendary magician Merlin.

Govan, not Glasgow?

Perhaps shockingly, to die hard Glasgow loyalists, historians think that Govan, on the south bank of the Clyde, close to the centre of today's Glasgow, was originally far more important than early settlements on the north bank, including those on the site now forming the heart of Glasgow city. The remains of an early Christian church with burials dating from between AD 400–600 have been found there, making it the earliest-known Christian site in the region. Legend says it was founded by St Ninian.

A later medieval chronicler claimed that King Constantine of Strathclyde, who ruled around AD 600, was converted to Christianity by St Columba, founded a monastery at Govan, gave up his kingdom to become a monk, and was himself honoured as a saint in a new church built there. But they might have been confusing him with other kings of the same name. Certainly, a wonderfully carved stone sarcophagus has been discovered at Govan. Produced around AD 1000, it might have been made to contain the relics of an earlier, honoured king. However, apart from the chronicler, we have no other evidence that Constantine ever existed...

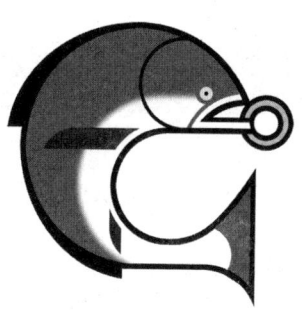

Homes for heroes?

The Govan tombstones are a collection of over 30 burial monuments, at Govan Church, dating from around AD 1000. They include 5 spectacular 'hogs-back' tombstones, richly decorated with Viking-style carvings. Experts think that they represent the curved roofs of great halls belonging to Viking chiefs, where they feasted with warriors after battle. Viking myths also tell how the brave continued feasting after death, in Valhalla, the hall of dead heroes. But these tombstones were carefully placed at a holy Christian site, and so the people buried beneath them were presumably also Christian. It seemed, however, that these Christians still remembered many pagan Viking traditions.

Mixed messages

So, the massive, magnificent Govan tombstones are Christian plus Viking. They were probably made for kings of Strathclyde, including a later namesake of the first, mysterious St

Constantine. But the story of contacts between Strathclyde kings and the Vikings begins many years before the tombstones were made.

Dumbarton Rock was sacked by Viking raiders based in Dublin in AD 870. After that, the Strathclyde kings moved inland for safety. Govan took over from Dumbarton Rock as their centre of government. The name Govan just possibly might refer to Owen the Bald, the last-known king of Strathclyde, who died in 1018.

After the raid in AD 870, the Vikings sailed home with 20 ships full of treasure. (Some of the most valuable cargo consisted of Scottish men, women and children, captured to be sold as slaves.) This tells us that the Strathclyde region had become rich, or at least rich enough to plunder and do business with.

However, the Govan tombstones suggest that, as well as fighting each other, Viking settlers and the Christian rulers and inhabitants of Strathclyde – especially Govan – also had more peaceful cultural, religious and economic contacts. Remains left by Viking raiders, traders and settlers in Strathclyde include coins, a broken sword, lead weights (probably used for weighing silver) and a splendid piece of jewellery – the Hunterston brooch – found in the Clyde estuary, near Largs. This was made in Ireland, decorated with a gold pattern copied from England. The owner's Gaelic name was scratched on the back, in Viking runes. Strathclyde was clearly a place where several cultures met – and mingled.

Mungo, myth and magic

All well and good for Govan. But what of Glasgow itself? While kings and Vikings were building, fighting and trading at Govan, on the opposite, northern bank of the Clyde, little fishing, farming, trading communities went on living much as they had done before.

Until, until? Remember the date! It's (probably) when Glasgow begins: AD 453. And remember, also, the Molendinar Burn from page 31? Well, according to legend – conveniently recorded for political purposes almost 400 years after the events it claims to describe – a certain St Mungo (c 518–603) is supposed to have founded a monastery about a kilometre above the place where the Molendinar flows into the Clyde, on the site of present-day Glasgow Cathedral. According to another later tradition, this was where Scotland's first saint, Ninian from Whithorn (d 432), had founded a Christian burial place.

Who was St Mungo?

Also known as St Kentigern (High Born), he was the son of Princess Theneu (who was later made a saint, too). She claimed to have been raped by a warrior prince visiting her father's court near Edinburgh. When her father discovered the pregnancy, he had Theneu thrown from a nearby high hill, Traprain Law. Miraculously she survived, and so her father had her set adrift in a boat, far out at sea. But again she did not die – early stories said God was looking after her. She landed near the site of modern Culross in Fife, where she was given shelter by a holy man, St Serf. She named her baby Kentigern; St Serf called him Mungo.

Theneu's name is still remembered in Glasgow, although in a rather peculiar way. 'St Teneu' has become 'St Enoch' – and a city-centre square, a grimy railway terminus, and a rather grim shopping centre have all been named after her. Poor St Teneu! Surely, she deserves better!

from schoolboy to saint

A confusing collection of legends and later stories tell us that Kentigern/Mungo was brought up by St Serf, who ran a monastery school. Once an adult, Mungo became a monk, and, around AD 550, was sent as a missionary to Strathclyde. There, he went to the house of a holy man, named Fergus. The same night, Fergus died and Mungo – miraculously – yoked two wild bulls to a cart and told them to carry Fergus to the place God had chosen. The bulls reached a low slope above the north bank of the River Clyde, close to a little salmon-fishing hamlet, and refused to go any further. Mungo buried Fergus there, calling the spot 'a dear green place'. Mungo also built a monastery next to Fergus's grave, close to an ancient (pagan) holy well. With the support of King Rhydderch Hael of Strathclyde, this became the centre of a new diocese (unit of church administration) with Mungo as its bishop (leader).

Around AD 560, it is said, Mungo had to flee from his dear green place. It was probably because local people wanted rid of Christian missionaries, though it is sometimes said that Mungo offended a powerful king. It's also said that he punished the king for over-taxing poor peasants by causing the River Clyde to rise and flood the royal barns, washing all the grain stored there up to Mungo's monastery. (Even if this story is not true, it suggests that local agriculture was flourishing, and may record an actual bad-weather event.) Mungo fled to Cumbria and Wales before returning to Galloway and then to the Glasgow basin – this time, the suburb of Kilmacolm. There, he met fellow-missionary St Columba (famous, among other achievements, for allegedly confronting the Loch Ness Monster). By now very aged, Mungo died in his bath* on 13th January AD 614. He was buried in the monastery church.

* This may possibly refer to a Christian baptism ceremony that Mungo was leading.

A saint and his symbols

You see them everywhere in Glasgow – at the City Chambers (magnificent Victorian home of Glasgow's governing council), at the University of Glasgow, in Glasgow's coat of arms, and even on lamp posts and bus shelters. Four special symbols: signs of St Mungo. They are listed in the rhyme on page 44. And there are many different versions of the stories that explain them:

There's the bird that never flew – a wild robin, tamed by St Serf. One of Mungo's classmates killed it, and blamed Mungo, but, by his prayers, Mungo brought the bird back to life again.

There's the bell that never rang – a handbell to call worshippers to Mungo's church, said to have been given to him by the Pope. It was treasured as a holy relic in medieval Glasgow. It disappeared sometime between 1578 and 1641.

There's the tree that never grew – as a young novice monk, Mungo was left to tend a holy fire. But he fell asleep and the other youngsters put out the fire, to get Mungo into trouble. But Mungo picked some ice-covered hazel twigs and prayed, and – alleluia – they burst into flames.

There's the fish that never swam – King Rhydderch Hael of Strathclyde gave a ring to his queen, Languoreth. The queen passed it on to her favourite knight, and this made the king jealous. While the knight was asleep, the king took the ring, and threw it into the River Clyde. Then he asked the queen to show him the ring; of course, she could not. Fearing for her life, the queen went to St Mungo. The saint sent one of his monks to the river, and told him to bring back the first fish he caught. It was a salmon – with the royal ring safe in its mouth!

Another saint – Valentine!

Since 1999, Glasgow has rather ambitiously been called 'the city of love' by some tour promoters. Why? Because of an arm-bone allegedly belonging to the famous late-Roman Christian martyr, St Valentine (d. AD 269). This relic currently resides in a peaceful little friary in a very poor part of Glasgow. People go to propose marriage in front of this relic, and the friars decorate it with red roses on St Valentine's Day.

A town is born!

At first, St Mungo's monastery was small. But slowly, Christianity became accepted in Strathclyde, and kings and church leaders came to rely on each other's support to maintain political and administrative power. Meanwhile, the saint and stories of his magic miracles proved increasingly popular. Mungo's fame – and his monastery – grew. The church there became a place of pilgrimage. Monks and pilgrims needed food, drink and shelter, so farming and fishing received a boost. Land was cleared for little fields and gardens between the monastery and fisheries on the River Clyde. Glasgow was beginning to grow.

New (royal) brooms

By around 1060, Church organisation in Scotland was being strengthened still further, thanks to the patronage of yet another saint, Queen Margaret, wife of Scottish king Malcolm III (ruled 1058–1093). She was by birth an Anglo-Saxon-Hungarian princess, and supported the continental, led-from-Rome strand of Christianity, not old-style Celtic worship as formerly practised in Scotland.

Malcolm III fought hard against Vikings in the north and Normans and English attacking from the south. His long reign did much to establish and secure the future for a new dynasty of Scottish kings who would rule a largely united kingdom of Scotland. The old Scottish kingdoms – including Strathclyde – faded away. So did Viking power.

Malcolm and Margaret's son, David I (ruled 1124–1153), continued their church and government policies. He gave generously to pay for church buildings, and encouraged others to do so. He also established burghs (approved, licensed towns), to promote trade, administration, law and order.

The old church centre at Govan was – in Malcolm and David's eyes – too closely linked with the kings of Strathclyde. It seemed sensible to start a new one at the dear green place: Glasgow! Around AD 1119 (dates vary) building work began to replace St Mungo's little monastery church with a much grander cathedral. King David himself attended the solemn consecration ceremony in 1136.

Blessed bones

Having a local saint already on the ground was a bonus, spiritually speaking, and also a way of attracting rich patrons. Later in the Middle Ages, St Mungo's shrine in Glasgow became the second most popular pilgrimage place in Scotland – and all Glasgow residents were required to pay their respects once a year at his tomb. No excuses accepted!

Business begins

Medieval bishops were powerful; as well as being spiritual leaders they were businessmen and politicians. Cathedrals were their headquarters. And so around Glasgow's new cathedral grew up houses for the cathedral staff and their servants, offices and a courthouse for the bishops' administrators, scribes, treasurers, lawyers and their visitors, plus a market to sell them food, drink and other necessities. A castle, where the bishop lived and entertained important visitors, was built. Church accommodation and offices were beside the new cathedral; the market was down by the river to make transport of goods easier.

Although Glasgow's bishops had influence all over the old kingdom of Strathclyde – and received rents and taxes from it – the town of Glasgow had no strong defences. In 1153 the Glasgow area was attacked by Norse/Scottish warlord Somerled, from his base on the island of Islay.

But Glasgow recovered and kept on growing. Around 1175, ambitious Bishop Jocelin was given royal permission to turn the town into a new-style burgh. Soon, markets and fairs brought more buyers and sellers – and money – to Glasgow. King David's grandson William 'the Lion'(or 'the Rough', depending on whose side you were on) granted a charter giving Glasgow the right to hold a weekly market. Later charters gave bishops further rights to administer weights and measures, punish thieves and fraudsters, and collect taxes. From 1190, Glasgow bishops won permission to hold an 8-day fair each July. Strangers – people from outside the burgh – could come to trade there, as well as local residents.

Glasgow fair

Until very recently, Glasgow Fair remained important as the main workers' holiday. Most shops and factories closed for a fortnight, and many families left the city to visit seaside resorts along the Clyde Estuary, or relatives in the Scottish countryside. 'Fair Monday' is still a public holiday in Glasgow today. But how many Glasgow residents taking the day off know that they're observing a tradition that is 800 years old?

Alas! They say if it rains on Fair Friday (at the start of the holiday) it will rain for the rest of the fortnight.

'A goodly city ... replenished well with all commodity [goods]...'

Army surveyor John Hardyng, in a report made for England's King Henry V, c. 1420

'Most renowned'

Glasgow markets and fairs prospered. After the end of the Middle Ages, Scottish Bishop John Leslie could boast, in 1578:

'Surely Glasgow is the most renowned market in all the west, honourable and celebrated... It is so frequent, and of such renown, that it sends to the Eastern countries [regions] very fat kye [cattle], herring likewise and salmon, ox-hides, wool and skins; butter, likewise, than which there is none better, and cheese. But, on the other hand, to the West (where there is a people very numerous in respect of the commodity [usefulness] of the sea coast), by other merchandise, all kind of corn to them sends.'

Church and Community in Medieval Glasgow, Histoire sociale-Social History, Vol. XV, No. 29 (mai-May 1982): 5–33, J. N. Miner.

Bigger and better

From the 13th century onwards, Glasgow grew fast. The new burgh developed around two focal points – the cathedral and its administrative centre on the hill, and the market down by the river. Along the streets linking the two – also along the street that ran east–west from rival towns Dumbarton and Lanark – there were burgage plots (houses with stables, storerooms, long gardens and orchards behind) laid out in well-planned order, with the wealthiest merchants' houses fronting the most important streets. Typically, houses had booths (shops) and counting houses (accounts offices) on the ground floor with accommodation on the upper storeys. Some had wooden balconies overlooking the street.

A muddy network of narrow vennels (pathways) ran behind and between the main streets. Craftsmen and women and other workers lived here with their families, in smaller houses and workshops. Houses, gardens and open areas of grassland used as pasture (for milk-cows and horses) were protected by wooden fences; main streets leading in and out of the burgh were barred by iron-studded wooden ports (gates). These were closed at night to keep out strangers, but also served in daytime as collecting points for tolls levied on goods entering Glasgow.

Town houses were made of wood and thatch, unlike the (more expensive) stone buildings close to the cathedral. Glasgow bishops borrowed money from bankers in Florence, Italy – the most financially advanced city in Europe – to help pay development costs. Most town residents did not own their homes but paid rent to the bishop or to the burgh council.

By 1285, Glasgow's first bridge spanned the Clyde, replacing the hazardous ford and the little boats that had ferried travellers over the river for millennia. In 1345, the timber bridge was replaced by a stone structure. Bridging the Clyde was a very considerable achievement; although the river was not deep, it was very wide (around 125 metres), and was bordered by treacherous sandbanks and mudflats. The cost in manpower and materials must have been enormous, the organisation very capable.

Early traders and craftworkers in the town, besides fishermen and farmers, included millers, bakers, cobblers and blacksmiths. They were soon joined by skinners, tanners, butchers, weavers and waulkers (who finished rough-woven cloth), cordiners (fine leatherworkers), hammer-makers and many more. Candle-makers supplied essential lighting for homes and shops, but were not allowed inside the burgh for fear of starting fires; the place where they lived and worked, just outside, is still known as 'Candleriggs' today.

Food, drink and goods produced in the town or brought in from the surrounding countryside were sold in Glasgow's many markets. At first, the market was held close to the cathedral, but as the lower areas of the town expanded, the market moved there, and diversified. By the 16th century, there were separate markets for fruit and vegetables (at Gallowgate), for fish (at the West Port), for meat, for oat and barley meal, for hay (essential for feeding horses) and for sour milk – the early Glasgow equivalent of yoghurt. Close to the river, there were 'dubs' (puddles) where geese were kept and fattened – then killed and sold for feathers and food.

Fresh water to drink (though it was probably safer boiled and made into weak ale) came from the Molendinar Burn, which flowed from close by the cathedral down along the eastern edge of the burgh. Water-powered mills gave the Molendinar its name and provided power to grind grain and for the fullers to shrink and polish woollen cloth. Travellers approaching the city from the east could also refresh themselves with pure water from the Lady Well – a spring just outside the burgh boundaries. (It still exists, and people drop coins into the water there – perhaps unwittingly continuing a pre-Christian tradition.)

Sited up at the top of the town, St Mungo's cathedral remained a building site for centuries. It was rebuilt twice after damaging fires; the west end was not completed until around 1350. In 1406, it was struck by lightning, and this meant further repairs. Inside, statues, decorated altars and fine stone carvings added to the building's beauty. Some of these were paid for by craft guilds, professional associations of expert craft-workers – another sign of Glasgow's growing sophistication and resources. All around the cathedral, fine large manses (stone homes) for cathedral officials were constructed; one of them – known as Provand's Lordship – is still standing. Apart from the cathedral, it is the oldest surviving complete building in Glasgow today.

Bishop's move?

During the Scottish Wars of Independence (against England) Bishop Wishart of Glasgow, who was in office from 1271 to 1316, took perhaps a rather too keen interest in the fighting. He was accused of diverting timber destined to be used for repairing the cathedral to make siege engines to fight against England's King Edward I. Nicknamed 'Hammer of the Scots', Edward had recently visited Glasgow to pay his respects at St Mungo's tomb and had given the wood as a religious offering. He did not expect it to be used by Scottish soldiers in their battles against him.

Late Medieval Glasgow map key

1. Cathedral Burying Ground
2. Glasgow Cathedral
3. Bishop's Castle
4. Blackadder's Hospital
5. St Nicholas' Hospital
6. Provand's Lordship
     (Glasgow's oldest surviving house)
7. Old Pedagogy (University lecture rooms)
8. Ladywell
9. University of Glasgow
10. Greyfriars Friary
11. Franciscan Friary
12. Grammar School
13. Dominican Friary
14. Blackfriars Friary
15. Little St Mungo's Chapel
16. East Port (gate)
17. Tolbooth
     (court-house and tax-collecting centre)
18. Mercat (merchants/market) Cross
19. Church of St Mary and St Anne
20. Tron Kirk (citizens' church)
21. West Port (gate)
22. Goose dubs (ponds and puddles)
23. Glasgow Green
24. Glasgow Bridge

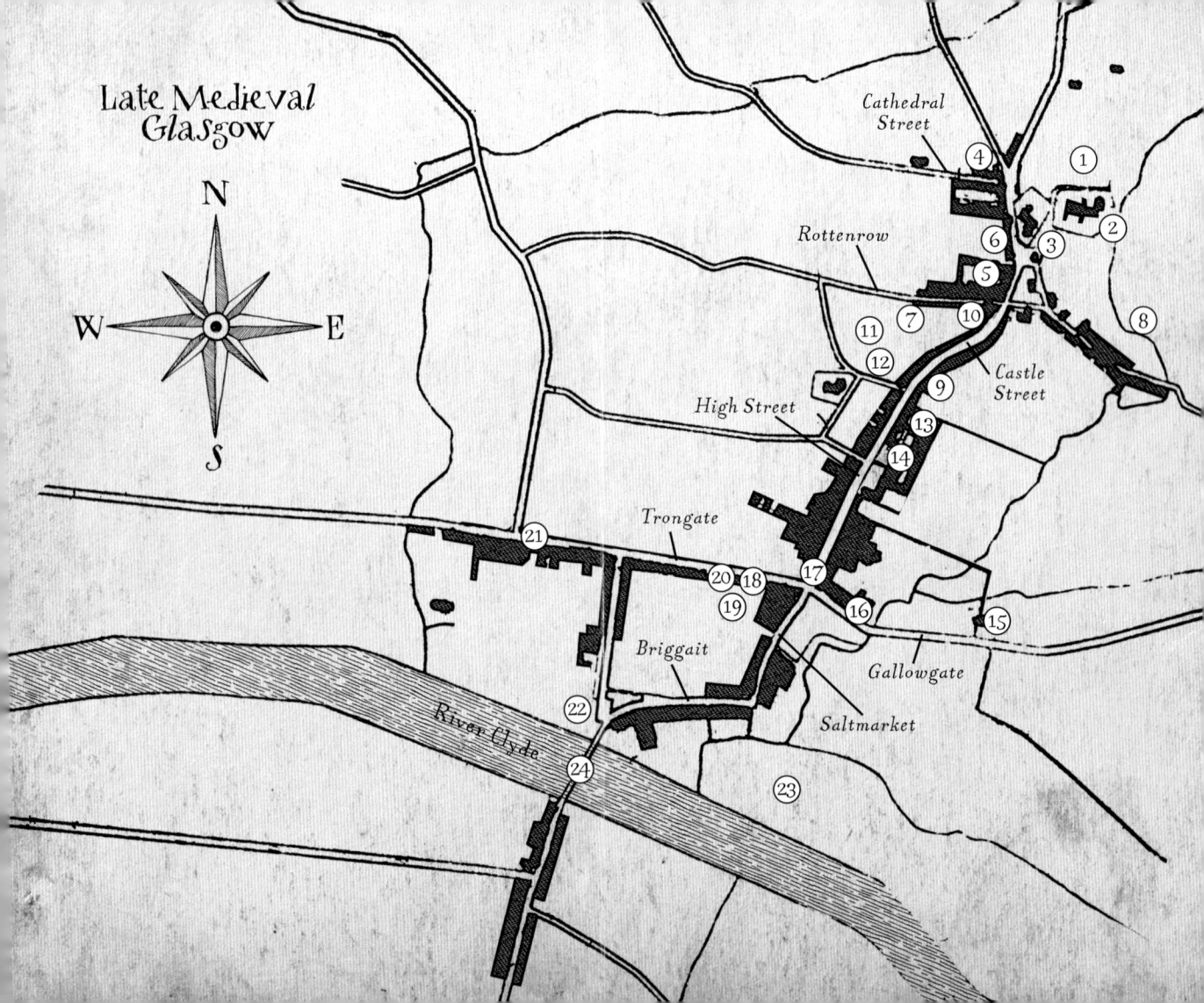

Late Medieval
Glasgow

N
W E
S

Cathedral
Street

①

④

②

⑥

③

⑤

Rottenrow

⑦ ⑩

⑪

⑫

⑨

⑧

Castle
Street

High Street

⑬

⑭

Trongate

㉑

⑳ ⑱

⑲

⑰

⑯

㉒

Briggait

㉔

River Clyde

Saltmarket

⑮

Gallowgate

㉓

Preaching and teaching

As Glasgow grew, the cathedral was joined by other religious institutions; in 1246, Dominican friars arrived to preach to the Glasgow townsfolk. Their church and friary occupied a large site on the east of today's High Street. In the 15th century, other brotherhoods of friars joined them. Rich Glaswegians gave money to build new churches in the lower town, including one in honour of St Teneu, founded in 1295. As a further sign of wealth and confidence, as well as piety, Glasgow residents also paid for a Leper House, outside the burgh boundaries, and, in 1464, for St Nicholas' Hospital – a refuge where people went to die in peace, rather than be cured of illness.

Churchmen were the most highly educated people in any medieval city, and provided all academic education in medieval Scotland. In 1451, scholarly, art-and-antiquity-loving Pope Nicholas V – a key figure in the Italian Renaissance – gave Glasgow's Bishop Turnbull permission to found a university, next to the Blackfriars. Nicholas was internationally famous. He was as powerful as a president today, and used to negotiating with kings and giving orders to armies. He was friends with Europe's top intellectuals, set up the world-class Vatican Library and saved many monuments and precious ancient texts from destruction. He was also passionate about promoting learning, which is probably why he encouraged the founding of the University of Glasgow; only the second to be set up in Scotland. But even so, it says something for Glasgow's rapidly advancing status that such an important – and far-away – figure as Pope Nicholas even knew that the burgh existed.

Around 1457, the original university buildings were expanded, and the 'Auld Pedagogy' (old learning centre) was added, to provide a lecture hall and student accommodation. Just three years later, a grammar school was founded, to teach children from Glasgow families.

Onwards and upwards

By around 1450, Glasgow had come a long, long way from those early fishermen's huts by the river. It was the richest, most important and powerful town in the west of Scotland, although richer cities and burghs (Aberdeen, Dundee) flourished in the east. As a religious centre, Glasgow was second only to the older and immensely prestigious St Andrews. To mark Glasgow's new spiritual – and economic and political – importance, Glasgow bishops were promoted to become archbishops in 1492. For them, and for Glasgow, this meant more power, more land and more money.

The REAL Blackadder

Yes, he existed. But he, Robert Blackadder, was not Rowan Atkinson in a multitude of disguises, but Glasgow's first archbishop. Born around 1455, he studied at the universities of St Andrews and Paris, then became a diplomat, carrying sensitive messages between Scottish kings and the Pope. After a time as an (unpopular) abbot in charge of the monastery at Melrose, he became bishop, then first-ever Archbishop, of Glasgow in 1492.

' Glasgow is, indeed,
a very fine city... '

*Daniel Defoe, novelist and
English government spy,
1707*

CHAPTER THREE

TROUBLES, TRIUMPHS – AND A WHIFF OF TOBACCO

Today, it's rare to meet a Glasgow resident who is not proud of their city in one way or another. It would probably have been the same in Glasgow in the mid-16th century. After suffering losses from repeated outbreaks of plague, most recently in 1504, Glasgow's population was recovering, reaching around 3,000 by the 1540s. At the same time, the city's wealth, mostly from trade, was growing, too; by 1557 it was among the top ten richest towns in Scotland. For many Glaswegians, the dear green place was – as it has been ever since – a place of enterprise and opportunity.

Glasgow was also making its voice heard beyond the old Strathclyde region. Glasgow merchants had won profitable rights to deal in foreign goods. The academics of the university were making exciting new contacts throughout Europe. By 1546, Glasgow was considered important enough to send a representative to the Scottish Parliament in Edinburgh.

Reflecting this confidence and prosperity, new buildings were springing up, or being rebuilt and repaired, all over the burgh: a new tron (official weighing station), a new tolbooth (council chamber and finance office, combined with a prison) and several new churches. The most important was St Mary's, built in 1525, under the patronage of burgh leaders. It became the 'town' church, used by people living in the trading streets of the burgh instead of the cathedral. Later in the 16th century, a clock (new technology!) and bell were added to the tolbooth; burgh gates were moved to make room for new houses, streets and vennels. Glasgow was getting bigger.

In 1524, a hospital (shelter) was founded by Roland Blackadder, nephew of Archbishop

Robert, 'for the support of poor and indigent coming into the city'. Like many other growing burghs, Glasgow was attracting men and women from the surrounding countryside, hoping to find work – or charity – there.

The great and the good

Glasgow was also developing a new 'personality', as an urban, commercial community, separate from the bishop and the cathedral. The first written record we have that mentions an independent burgh council is dated 1501, though a ruling group of sorts had probably existed for at least a century before that. Council members were led by a provost (senior magistrate; in modern terms, the chief executive of the burgh), assisted by two bailies (junior magistrates, who also held the keys to the city ports). All three were appointed by the archbishop, who chose the provost from the local gentry, and the bailies from Glasgow men recommended by burgh councillors.

The councillors themselves were respected and respectable Glasgow residents; most were merchants or senior craftsmen. Existing councillors chose new members to replace those who had died or were retiring.

By 1559, the city's craft guilds, which regulated quality standards and organised apprenticeships to train youngsters in skilled occupations, had also joined together into a corporation. By 1605, these had merged with the burgh council to create a formidable network of Glasgow's most influential people.

Glasgow magistrates

No, not the burgh council but the strange nickname for salted herring, caught from the deep waters of Loch Fyne that flows into the Firth of Clyde and sold in Glasgow market. It was traditionally eaten as a 'meridian' (lunchtime snack) with a pint of ale, or at supper time with bread and a soft boiled egg. The name may come from the fact that all Glasgow products – even smelly salt fish – had to be inspected by magistrates before they could be put on sale.

And speaking of ale...

Brewing was first recorded on the banks of the Molendinar Burn in 1556. Today the same site, plus the surrounding land, is still used for the same purpose, though the site is now known as the Wellpark Brewery. Since 1740, it has been occupied by Scotland's largest brewery business, Tennent's. The company first made its fortune in the 19th century, when Tennent's was the world's largest exporter of bottled beer – using Clyde-built ships, of course.

Clouds on the horizon

So there was progress. Lots of progress. But more than a few Glasgow men or women might also have been feeling a little bit uneasy. Why? Because, in spite of Glasgow's growing wealth and confidence, the years that lay ahead were troubled times indeed. The problems were religion and politics. When combined, they whipped up a storm. Throughout Europe, Protestant religious reformers were challenging the authority and some of the doctrines of the Roman Catholic Church. They wanted freedom to worship in the way they thought best – and to escape from control by the Pope in Rome. Closer to home, relations between Scotland and its stronger, richer neighbour England were rapidly deteriorating.

In 1508, the burgh council defied the archbishop's right to appoint all grammar-school masters – teachers who would shape the views of the next generation of Glasgow citizens – and appointed a candidate of their own. In 1528, Archbishop James Beaton, who had recently moved from Glasgow to St Andrews, gave orders to burn a Protestant preacher as a heretic. In 1559, friar Jeremy Russell was hanged in Glasgow for his Protestant beliefs, and the same year, the Greyfriars church and friary, at the top of Glasgow High Street, was looted by troops working for powerful Protestant nobles.

In spite of these quarrels, 16th-century Glasgow was a safer place to live than bigger, richer eastern cities, such as Edinburgh and Dundee. Because of their position and their wealth, they were more likely to be attacked by

English invaders, especially during the 'Rough Wooing' of 1543–1551, when King Henry VIII of England sent invading armies to Scotland, in a (failed) bid to force a marriage between his son Edward VI and young Mary Queen of Scots.

Later, the target of those invasions, romantic Queen Mary of Scots herself, visited Glasgow in January 1567 and stayed in Provand's Lordship (see page 68), close to the cathedral. Henry Darnley, her handsome, dissolute husband, 'sick of the pox', was banished to stay in a smaller house nearby. He was murdered in Edinburgh just a few weeks later. It was said that Mary wrote one or more of the incriminating 'Casket Letters' (see page 80) during her stay in Glasgow. But this may not be true.

'Things not heard of before'

Not long before Queen Mary's visit, in 1560, the Scottish Parliament, meeting in Edinburgh, made a momentous decision. It declared that the Church throughout Scotland should be reformed, and break away from the Catholic

Church of Rome. This was a revolution – not only in religious beliefs and ways of worship, but also in international politics, Church organisation and education. As Edinburgh Professor Tom Devine explained in 2010: 'The Reformation was a defining moment for us as a people.' Scotland – and Glasgow – would never be the same again.

Did she or didn't she?

The Casket Letters are eight letters plus a few poems that were alleged to have been written by Mary Queen of Scots early in 1567 to James Bothwell, Lord High Admiral of Scotland, plotting her husband's murder. They were used in evidence against Mary by Scottish lords, who wanted to make her give up her throne in favour of her infant son.

The letters could well have been forgeries, designed to discredit Mary. But she and Bothwell married only a few weeks after Darnley's death. Just one month later, in June 1567, Mary was forced to abdicate, and her son, James VI, became king.

Glasgow played a leading part in this cultural revolution. The property and legal rights belonging to Glasgow's Cathedral and archbishop passed to the new, Calvinist Church of Scotland. The last Roman Catholic Archbishop of Glasgow until modern times, James Beaton, fled to France in 1560.

faith and destiny

Scottish Protestants, led by fiery preacher John Knox, were strongly influenced by the ideas of French reformer, Jean Calvin (1509–1564), especially predestination: the belief that everything that happens is God's will, so some people are destined to be good, and others to be sinners. Linked to this, they also believed that the Church should not be led by priests and bishops but governed by assemblies of good, faithful believers.

'Times of trouble and danger'

- **1560s** Friars, monks, priests and grammar-school headmaster flee. Religious property sold. Blackfriars is given to the University of Glasgow; Greyfriars is taken over by the burgh council. The 'sang chool' (choir school) at Glasgow Cathedral becomes a primary school.

- **1579** Protestant reformers plan to demolish the cathedral. Glasgow craftsmen riot; it is saved.

- **1610** General Assembly of Church of Scotland reintroduces bishops; many Scots disapprove.

- **1615** Priest John Ogilvie is hanged in Glasgow for saying Roman Catholic Mass.

- **1638** General Assembly of Church held in Glasgow votes to abolish bishops.

- **1639–1653** Covenanters (strict Presbyterians) grow stronger; royal troops hunt them down. Glasgow supports Covenanters and is occupied by royal army, but is not sacked. (It pays a heavy fine instead.)

- **1645** Royalist General Montrose occupies Glasgow; celebrates victory over Covenanters. He calls Scottish Parliament to meet there: a sign of Glasgow's growing importance.

- **1650** Lord Protector Oliver Cromwell visits Glasgow, hunting supporters of exiled King Charles II.

- **1660** Monarchy restored in England. New King Charles II wants bishops.

- **1662** Bishops reintroduced. Archbishop back in Glasgow. The provost, burgh council and many Glasgow citizens are angry.

- **1669** Scottish Parliament says that kings can appoint bishops / control Church. Archbishop Burnet of Glasgow resigns in protest.

- **1675** Glasgow bans radical Protestant prayer meetings. These are later allowed, but only outside the burgh.

- **1688/9** King James VII/II escapes to exile; Protestants William and Mary of Orange become the English monarchs. Scottish Church abolishes bishops (again).

- **1690** End of bishops' control of Glasgow city.

New ideas

Religious upheavals also led to a remarkable renewal for the University of Glasgow. Strange but true: religious intolerance and a love for new, rational, non-religious ideas flourished in the same place and at the same time.

In the early 1560s, when Catholic priests and scholars were dismissed from their positions, the university almost collapsed. Mary Queen of Scots gave money to support it. Then, in 1570, Calvinist reformer and brilliant scholar Andrew Melville (1545–1622) returned from religious exile in Calvin's model Protestant community of Geneva to become university principal.

Another revolution! Melville introduced a whole new programme of study, based on Protestant beliefs and Renaissance ideas and discoveries: history, geography, philosophy, mathematics, astronomy, Ancient Greek, science and literature. Just as importantly, Melville encouraged a new, science-friendly approach to education. Glasgow students learned to criticise and ask questions and to challenge old beliefs and ideas.

The university never looked back. Soon professors were complaining that it was 'standing room only'; the new lectures were attracting crowds of students. The Glasgow approach to learning and the curriculum were influential throughout Scotland. Glasgow-trained scholars pioneered a new, rational approach in many subjects, especially law and philosophy, and led research into scientific and practical subjects. The most famous Glasgow graduate was probably Adam Smith (1723–1790), still influential today as 'the father of economics'.

'Cleanest and best-built'

In 1707 English novelist and spy Daniel Defoe came to Glasgow. He called it the 'cleanest and best-built city in Britain' outside London. Defoe was fortunate to visit at a time when new buildings were replacing old medieval structures destroyed in two damaging fires (1652 and 1677). But he was right. Glasgow was becoming very fine. Very fine indeed. Defoe described not one but four principal streets lined with stone-built houses, a spacious market place, the long, high River Clyde bridge and a new merchants' meeting house that was 'very noble and strong'.

He declared that the university buildings were 'the best of any in Scotland' and that the cathedral spire was 'very handsome'.

Perhaps most important of all, Defoe defined Glasgow as 'a city of business'. That's where the money came from to pay for all the new buildings. It's estimated that there were about 400 merchants in Glasgow around 1680, out of a population of roughly 12,000. Among the crowded shops, markets and workshops,

Lovely linen

Linen is woven from fibres from the flax plant, which grows well in cool, damp Scotland. From the 1680s, to encourage the linen industry, all Scots had by law to be buried in Scottish-made linen shrouds. In 1748, linen was further boosted by a ban on the import of French cambric – a fine fabric used for clothing. By 1770, Glasgow spinners and weavers produced more linen than any other city in the UK. Spinners and weavers both worked at home, on hand- and foot-powered machines; their raw materials and finished work were supplied and collected by merchants.

Defoe noted 'handsome sugar-baking houses' that turned molasses from America and the Caribbean into high-price refined sugar, and a distillery that made 'Glasgow Brandy' (a type of rum). He admired Glasgow salted herring, saying it was 'as good as Dutch'. And he remarked upon made-in-Glasgow colourful woollen plaid cloth, worn as shawls by Scottish women, 'a habit peculiar to the country'. He also noted the fashionable Glasgow muslins, gloves and lots and lots of linen.

Glasgow punch

This drink was enjoyed in Glasgow and elsewhere in Scotland from around 1700–1900. Apart from the water – ideally from a spring – it was entirely made of ingredients imported to Glasgow from America and / or the Caribbean: rum, sugar, lemon and limes.

Its effects were not always admired: 'Mistress Meg Dods' (a pen-name), who wrote *The cook and housewife's manual* published in Edinburgh in 1826, describes it as 'A treacherous and detestable liquor.'

Glasgow businesses begin

- 1625 New quay for unloading cargo built at Broomielaw.
- 1636 First printing business in Glasgow.
- 1638 First wool 'manufactory' (organised weaving workshop); also many small businesses making useful goods such as soap and woollen bonnets. Glasgow businesses also include gold-workers, a clockmaker, a coppersmith and a pewterer, plus makers / processors of salt, butter, herring, oats and meal, paper, coal, timber and many kinds of animal hides.
- 1660 First-known coal pit (mine) in Gorbals district.
- 1662 First post office in Glasgow.
- 1667 New soapworks and associated whaling boats (the whale oil was used in soap).
- 1667 First sugar refinery.
- 1673 First Coffee House in Glasgow.
- 1674 Tobacco first imported to Glasgow.
- 1678 First stagecoaches, to Edinburgh.
- 1690 First branch of Bank of Scotland in Glasgow.
- 1715 *Glasgow Courant* newspaper first published.

- 1719 Cotton printing businesses begin.
- 1729 *Glasgow Journal* newspaper first published.
- 1730 New glassworks, to make bottles for exported beer.
- 1735 Glasgow shipowners have 67 registered ships; there is also a lot of smuggling.
- 1736 Glasgow now has ropeworks, tanneries and ironworks making everything from delicate locks to massive anchors, and two tobacco factories.
- 1740 About 685,000 square metres of linen woven every year in Glasgow.
- 1742 Dutch-style 'delft' pottery made in Glasgow.
- 1749 Glasgow's own bank opens (Dunlop, Houston & Co). Known as the 'ship bank' because it loans money to build ships and finance trading voyages.
- 1751 John Smith bookshop opens (and is still running).
- 1750 Ribbon-weaving works (ribbons fastened clothes, as well as decorating them).
- 1753 Glasgow–Edinburgh road becomes a turnpike (well-maintained toll-road).
- 1769 Imported cotton first spun and woven in Glasgow.

Disaster at Darien (1698-1700)

It was not all plain sailing for Glasgow business people. Unwise investments could ruin an enterprise overnight. In the late 1690s, many Glasgow investors lost all their money in the ill-fated Darien scheme. This was a plan to set up a Scottish colony called Caledonia at Darien in Panama, to handle trade across the Atlantic and the Pacific oceans. From the start, the Darien project was hampered by poor planning. The English blockaded the colony; the Spanish attacked it. Some colonists died from injuries, but many, many more were killed by tropical diseases. The scheme was a disaster, and the plan was abandoned.

United we stand?

Defoe also observed, correctly, that Glasgow's overseas trade was just as important as its trade with the rest of Scotland and England, adding that Glasgow was the only city in Scotland where both types of trade were increasing. The Union of the Crowns in 1603 had opened up the English market to Glasgow traders. Glasgow ships sailed south to ports along Britain's west coast – and then ventured further, to Portugal, Spain and other Mediterranean countries. As Defoe noted, Glasgow's western situation gave it a competitive advantage over Scotland's east-coast ports. West-coast shipping also escaped attack from pirates that 'thronged' (Defoe) the English Channel, and preyed on ships from London and south-coast ports.

After the Act of Union between England and Scotland in 1707, Glasgow was even more advantageously placed to profit from trade across the Atlantic with England's colonies and plantations in America and the Caribbean. Not so much 'bought and sold for English gold' (Robert Burns) as 'saved by English silver'. The Union opened up what had been

Get rich quick –
the Glasgow business model

Capital accumulated from trade was invested in new industry.

The profit was invested in new ships, new trading ventures to new places, new industries – and fine city buildings.

The manufactured goods were then exported to new markets, generating profit.

English-only markets to Scottish traders, tax-free. Glasgow's transatlantic trade became so successful that rival English ports complained to the London Parliament that the Scots were not playing fair.

Even so, many Scots bitterly resented the loss of Scottish sovereignty. (And you thought Brexit was bad...) There were anti-Union protests and riots in Glasgow in 1707 and again close by in Shawfield in 1725, when nine protesters were killed.

Bonnie Charlie's noo awa!

The Union of 1707 was followed by a series of Jacobite rebellions. Glasgow was not Jacobite – merchants knew which side their bannocks were buttered – and few rich Glasgow women flirted with romantic rebellious ideas, unlike fine Edinburgh ladies. When Bonnie Prince Charlie (Charles Edward Stuart, the son of exiled King James VII) visited Glasgow, on Christmas Day 1745, he was not made very welcome. He was offered hospitality in Glasgow's finest house, Shawfield Mansion (and met his new Scottish mistress there), but feared to venture out, saying that he had never before felt so much 'without friends'. Glasgow provost Buchanan joked grimly that he was more afraid of upsetting his fellow Glaswegians than of the prince's Highland army which was camped on Glasgow Green.

Charles ordered the Glasgow magistrates, on pain of death, to supply his army with 12,000 shirts and 6,000 cloth coats, pairs of stockings and waistcoats. It says much for the wealth of Glasgow, and the volume of its manufacturing industries, that the magistrates were able to satisfy Charles' demands, albeit reluctantly.

New Port, Lang Dyke

In 1668, a new harbour – Newport Glasgow (later, simply Port Glasgow) – was built on the south shore of the Clyde, close to the river estuary. It was designed to serve as a deep-water port where large sailing ships could dock and offload their cargoes. Freight was transhipped into smaller, shallow-draught boats, which ferried it up the Clyde to Glasgow, or carried there by horse and cart.

Glasgow's main Custom House (to collect import duties and tolls) was moved to Port Glasgow in 1710. Shipbuilding began at Port Glasgow in 1762. There were also dry-docks, for ship repairs.

Port Glasgow was extremely useful; in fact, it was essential for Glasgow's transatlantic trade. But the basic problem remained. The River Clyde close to Glasgow was too shallow for ocean-going shipping, because of sandbanks and shoals. In 1768, the Clyde was narrowed by building jetties along its banks. It was hoped that the river waters would wash away sand and gravel as they forced their way through the narrows, creating a deeper channel. In 1773, a long wall, called the Lang Dyke, was built in the river near the Clyde estuary, for the same purpose. These schemes worked, but the Clyde was not safe or easy for large ships to navigate until millions of tonnes of silt was removed in the mid and late 19th century by mechanical dredgers.

A place of my own

In 1670, around 14,000 people lived in Glasgow. By the 1750s, the population had risen to over 23,000. Much of the open space within the old burgh was being built on. Overcrowding threatened! Enterprising landowners living in the countryside nearby saw an opportunity. They would build new settlements where workers could live, free of rules and regulations imposed by Glasgow's old craft guilds. The landowners would profit from rents paid for homes and factories; the workers could sell their products in Glasgow.

The first of these suburbs was Calton, founded in 1705. It was soon followed by many other developments. One of the best-known began as rows of weavers cottages built by the Anderson family, close to what is now the northern end of the Kingston Bridge across the Clyde. In 1735, they sold it to an ambitious entrepreneur, who set up dyeing, bleaching and cloth-printing works on the banks of the river. He soon added glassworks, a new pottery works (there had been one at Calton since the 1590s) and a brewery. By 1791, about 4,000 people lived in Anderston. Nearby Finnieston, founded in 1768, developed in a similar way.

What about the workers?!

In 1787, the new suburb of Calton was the site of Scotland's first industrial dispute when 7,000 weavers, members of the Clyde Weavers' Association, went on strike to protest against a 25% cut in their wages. Troops were sent in, and three people were killed. The leader, James Granger, was sentenced to be flogged.

Tobacco barons and sugar daddies

By the 1770s, tobacco was Glasgow's largest industry. Grown on American plantations, such as Virginia, dried tobacco leaves were carried to Scotland in Glasgow ships, processed in Glasgow factories (often by child workers), then exported all over Europe. Glasgow Tobacco Barons grew enormously rich and became the burgh's elite. They met to discuss business and drink claret in Glasgow's splendid Merchants' Hall, built new churches and lived in fine new mansions (in what's now known as Merchant City district, to the west of old Glasgow). Glasgow place names, such as Virginia Street, still record their influence. And a magnificent mansion, built for tobacco merchant William Cunninghame, still survives (though it's been extended), and is now Glasgow's Gallery of Modern Art. Like other respectable Glasgow citizens, the tobacco barons wore sober dark clothes – but liked to cover them with flamboyant scarlet cloaks and carry walking canes topped with real gold.

Glasgow was Europe's most important tobacco port; by the 1770s imports totalled almost 20 million kilos each year. Sugar, grown on plantations in the Caribbean, was almost as important. You can read more about Glasgow's 'sugar daddies' – and their infamous Pig Club on pages 105–106.

On their outward journeys to America, tobacco ships carried cargoes of Glasgow-made goods, and also items made elsewhere in Britain, for sale to colonists. This included everything that might possibly be useful, from woollen or linen cloth, knitted stockings and leather shoes to bottled beer and salt herring. Glasgow ships also carried timber, iron and rope for house and ship building – and another, shameful cargo: African slaves.

Not~so~secret shame

To put it bluntly, slavery made 18th-century Glasgow rich. Ships carrying slaves rarely docked at Glasgow, but Glasgow ships sailed to Africa laden with goods to exchange for slaves, and Glasgow merchants and shipowners supplied almost everything that slave-owners in America and the Caribbean needed to live, work and prosper. And Glasgow workers made it. All this wealth was in addition to the phenomenal profits made by the sale of sugar and tobacco grown on slave plantations.

There was even more. Glasgow's shipping and shipbuilding industries, its docks and warehouses, its outlying harbours at Port Glasgow and Greenock, and its carter and carriers, horse-breeders and cart-builders all shared in the wealth made from supplying slave-owners. And where did they, like all other Glasgow workers, spend this money? In Glasgow's markets, shops and taverns, and by paying rent to Glasgow landlords, or by commissioning new homes, gardens, workshops and warehouses from Glasgow builders.

Servants – and slaves

Across the Atlantic, Glaswegians worked on plantations as managers, clerks and accountants. Men and women from poor Glasgow families also volunteered to go to the colonies as indentured servants. They were bound to work for a master there for a set number of years – and then free to try to start to make a new life for themselves in the 'New World'. Most emigrant Glaswegians were ambitious, and hoped one day to have a plantation of their own. Scots masters had a terrible reputation for harshness. In Jamaica, for example, where one in three plantations was Scots-owned, a slave's life expectancy was a pitiful four years. Slaves were disposable; a commodity. It was cheaper to buy a new slave than to treat existing slaves humanely.

Slave-owning was banned in Scotland in 1778, and throughout most British colonies in 1807. Although quite a few Glasgow families had slaves and servants of African origin – black faces would have been quite a familiar sight in the streets of Glasgow – many of the burgh's merchants played a leading part in

The charms of the Indies

Robert Burns – the poor ploughman, the rebellious spirit, the poet of the people! But also a man of his times. Although Burns later lamented the shocking state of slaves on a ship he saw in Dundee, in his youth, before he was famous, he made plans to go to the Caribbean to work as a clerk on a slave plantation.

After a whirlwind romance, in 1786 he invited one of his very many girlfriends to elope with him:

'Will ye go to the Indies, my Mary,
And leave auld Scotia's shore?
Will ye go to the Indies, my Mary,
Across th' Atlantic roar?

O sweet grows the lime and the orange,
And the apple on the pine;
But a' the charms o' the Indies
Can never equal thine...'

the campaign to abolish slavery, most notably sugar-merchant James MacDowall, who was provost in 1795.

Is this the end?

Economically speaking, in the 1770s Glasgow's future, especially if viewed through a puff of tobacco smoke, seemed rosy – and secure. But in 1776 what happened? Yes, the United States' Declaration of Independence! British imports (they included Scotland's, too) were rejected by rebel colonists. Rebel soldiers disrupted on-land tobacco production, while rebel warships attacked ships at sea and blockaded colonial ports. Glasgow's tobacco trade was ruined. The city's wealth was in danger. What could save it?

Look thro' the town, the houses here
Like noble palaces appear:
A' things the face o' gladness wear –
The market's thrang,
(crowded)
Bis'ness is brisk, and a's asteer
(buzzing)
The streets alang!
(along)

Clean-keepit streets! sae lang and braid,
(broad)
The distant objects seem to fade!
And then for shelter, or for shade,
Frae sun or show'r,
Piazzas lend their friendly aid,
At ony hour!

From Glasgow, A Poem *by John Mayne, 1783*

CHAPTER FOUR

'METROPOLIS OF THE WEST'*

W ho sipped turtle soup, munched roast suckling pig, placed extravagant bets on card games (or on the outcome of battles fought against Napoleon), got drunk on rum punch and wore a heavy chain necklace with a silver pig pendant? The president of Glasgow's exclusive Pig Club, a once-a-week members-only gathering of top sugar merchants and their friends. Founded in 1798 and holding its last meeting in 1807 (the year the slave trade was banned in British colonies), the Pig Club represented Glasgow's merchant elite at the end of the 18th century. And it reflected their interests: money-making, Tory-party politics – and Glasgow's future.

* A well-known term of praise for Glasgow, used in the late 18th and early 19th centuries.

As well as spending lavishly on food and drink, and on holding balls in Glasgow's elegant new Assembly Rooms – 400 dancers from Glasgow's leading families would regularly attend – Pig Club members also gave generously to Glasgow charities. It was needed; city business had slumped. We saw how the American Revolution of 1776 halted Glasgow's tobacco trade almost overnight. What saved Glasgow – the 'metropolis of the west' – was the rapid growth of the trade in sugar imported from the Caribbean, together with the export of Glasgow-made and Scottish goods to Caribbean sugar plantations.

King Cotton

Sugar was a short-term fix. Long after 1800, the sugar trade continued to make money, but cotton proved to be a bigger and better foundation for Glasgow's economic future. It was grown first in the Caribbean and then in the USA after independence, but spun, woven and printed in Scotland. Cheap 'slave goods' (clothes and shoes) were made in Glasgow, too. By around 1820, Glasgow cottons were being sold to India, and soon afterwards to China and Australia. From around 1830, Glasgow ships also carried colonists to southern Africa and the Pacific region.

The expansion of new markets in other British colonies, especially in Canada, also boosted Glasgow's trade. Big, fast, strong ships (often American-made) belonging to Glasgow merchants sailed west laden with cotton fabrics, household goods and all kinds of domestic necessities; they also carried many thousands of emigrants from Scotland to the 'New World'. They returned laden with raw cotton, sugar, coffee, spices, raw materials for medicines and vast quantities of Canadian timber. This was urgently needed to build new homes, factories, workshops, canals, railways and machines, as Britain's population, towns and industries all expanded.

Nearer home, Glasgow became the centre for trade in every imaginable kind of commodity for the whole of western Scotland and the Isles. It was also Ireland's most important trading partner. And, once canals linked Glasgow to east Scotland and the North Sea (from the 1790s), Glasgow became the leading port handling the sale of American colonial goods to continental Europe, and was able to import coal, flax and timber from Baltic lands and Scandinavia.

In the 1770s, work had begun on two new waterways that would connect the east and west coasts of Scotland, and important mining or manufacturing places in between. The Monkland Canal ran from Coatbridge to eastern Glasgow; the Forth and Clyde ran between Glasgow and Grangemouth near Edinburgh. A third canal was planned but never completed; it ran south of the Clyde and was intended to have linked Glasgow with the Ayrshire coast.

The dream...

'Could this city [Glasgow] but have a communication with the Firth of Forth [on the east coast of Scotland]... they would in a few years double their trade.'

Daniel Defoe, 1707

... and the reality

To gi'e her inland trade a heeze, (boost)
As weel's her foreign,
She's join'd the East and Western Seas
Together, roaring!

From Glasgow, A Poem *by John Mayne, 1783*

'United we stand'

Like other trading centres throughout
Europe, Glasgow's shipping and businesses
were disrupted by blockades and sea battles
during the wars against Revolutionary
and Napoleonic France (1792–1815). But
Glasgow's concentration on Atlantic sea routes
made its shipping less likely to be attacked.
Glasgow's merchants and traders also joined
together to protect their joint interests and
plan new enterprises. Glasgow Chamber of
Commerce, founded in 1783, was the first in
Britain. Soon after, it was joined by West India
and East India trading associations.

At the same time, Glasgow's population soared, mostly through immigration from the surrounding countryside and from western Scotland. From maybe 30,000 in 1770 it increased to 200,000 by around 1830. By the 1820s, Glasgow was bigger than Edinburgh. It was – and remains – Scotland's biggest city.

Rich and poor

Glasgow's new wealth was not evenly distributed. While members of the Pig Club and their friends feasted, danced and lived in elegant new mansions, many – perhaps most – ordinary families lived in damp, cold, thatched cottages or garrets, crowded into just one or two rooms. Often, living and sleeping areas served as workplaces as well, with hand-looms and spinning wheels taking up a lot of the space. Heating (if any) came from open wood or coal fires, which were also used for cooking. If a fire was not possible, take-away food – typically hot pies – could be bought from shops and stalls. Lighting was a tallow 'dip', bedcovers were sacks or old clothes. Water was carried from public wells and there were no lavatories. As the population grew

Glasgow grows...

New homes, workshops, docks and factories were built on both banks of the Clyde.

Across the river...

'Glasgow is divided by the river Clyde into two un-equal parts, that portion occupying the northern bank being the chief: this comprehends the old and new towns...'

Pigot and co.'s commercial directory of... Scotland, and of the Isle of Man, *1837*

And into the country

'The suburbs of Glasgow extend very far, houses on each side of the highway – all ugly, and the inhabitants dirty. The roads are very wide; and everything seems to tell of the neighbourhood of a large town. We were annoyed by carts and dirt, and the road was full of people... the children often sent a hooting after us.'

Recollections of a Tour Made in Scotland, *Dorothy Wordsworth, 1803*

and Glasgow became ever more crowded, the pool of available labour increased, wages and payments for piecework fell and the Glasgow poor became poorer.

Yes, it really existed: cow-heel pie*

'...the Bridgegate has been celebrated for the quality of its Tripe, Potted-Meat, and Cow-Heel. Even the most fashionable Famulies used regularly to send to the Bridgegate for their supply of Tripe; and thousands of Convivial Parties have regaled themselves on this Dish upon the Spot, followed by libations of Glasgow Punch or Whisky Toddy...'

History of Glasgow from the earliest to the present times by Writers of Eminence, *edited and published by John Tweed, Glasgow, 1873*

* Beloved of children's comic character Desperate Dan, created for Dundee publishers DC Thomson.

'All human life is there...'

What was this fast-changing city like as a place to live? Well, browsing through old trade directories can be like travelling back in time. There they are, neatly arranged: facts and figures about past city streets and their inhabitants, plus some rather unexpected details.

In 1837, for example, we can read that there were regular mail services from Glasgow to almost anywhere in the world, including China, Australia and Chile. Noisy and dirty Glasgow might have been, but it was very well connected! And – those were the days – Glasgow post offices stayed open until 10 pm, Monday to Saturday.

Directories tell us that, in the early 1800s, there was a Glasgow Zoo (however, the poor exhibits were 'chiefly stuffed'), that the University had an astronomical observatory for studying the skies and an anatomical theatre where dead bodies were publicly dissected, that a horse-drawn railway (the Garnkirk and Glasgow) opened in 1831, bringing coal, and that the bold businessman who smuggled Britain's first inkle-weaving looms to Glasgow from the Netherlands in 1732 risked death to do so. (Inkles were ribbons and braids; essential at a time when zips, Velcro™ and elastic had not yet been invented, and also used to decorate male and female clothing.)

We learn, too, that Glasgow had numerous coffee shops (sounds modern, but they were for men only; they went to discuss business and read newspapers) and a second-hand bookshop, several trunk-makers and a specialist pencil-maker. Oh, and that the crypt (underground room) beneath the cathedral, full of medieval bones, was an 'appalling' and scary spectacle.

Getting and spending...

The directories also tell us that if we strolled through Glasgow's main streets and squares, and the tangle of smaller roads, wynds, vennels, courts and closes that connected them, we would find a tremendous variety of businesses, mostly small, but several large and impressive.

In the early 18th century, most people did their shopping at Glasgow's markets (the main market day was Wednesday). They bought rare or novelty items from travelling pedlars or at July's Glasgow Fair. But fixed shops – mostly just rooms in city tenements – steadily grew more popular, and by 1830 there were over 500 such shops in Glasgow. Scotland's first shopping arcade opened in Argyle Street in 1826, and by around the same date there were permanent stalls at Candleriggs selling perishable foods such as poultry, eggs, butter, cheese and vegetables.

Mixed in among these new shops were workshops producing cheap everyday items and the finest of furnishings. In Glasgow's damp, cool climate, warm clothes were a priority, but for those who could afford it, style was important, too. Directories list makers and sellers of women's dresses, men's tailoring, boots, shoes, stockings, hats, shawls and corsets as well as the 'pirated' inkle braids and ribbons. There were hairdressers, soap-makers and perfumiers – and a portrait-painter, to record the finished 'look'.

Home-workers

In ilka house, frae man to boy,   (each)
A' hands, in Glasgow, find employ:
Ev'n little maids, wi' meikle joy,   (little)
Flow'r lawn and gauze,   (embroider)
Or clip, wi' care, the silken soy   (silk satin)
For Ladies' braws.   (finery)

Their fathers weave, their mothers spin,
The muslin robe, sae fine and thin,
That, frae the ancle to the chin,
It aft discloses
The beauteous symmetry within –
Limbs, neck and bozies!

From Glasgow, A Poem *by John Mayne, 1783*

116

The talk of the steamie

Dirty clothes and household linens were washed, by professional washerwomen or poor housewives, on Glasgow Green, a large open space on the banks of the Clyde, south-east of the cathedral. The washing was then spread out on the grass to bleach and dry.

'This field, the whole summer through, is covered with women of all ages, children, and young girls spreading out their linen, and watching it while it bleaches.

In the middle of the field is a wash-house, whither the inhabitants of this large town, rich and poor, send or carry their linen to be washed. There are two very large rooms, with each a cistern in the middle for hot water; and all round the rooms are benches for the women to set their tubs upon. Both the rooms were crowded with washers; there might be a hundred, or two, or even three...'

Dorothy Wordsworth, Recollections of a Tour Made in Scotland, *1803*

'Steamie' = communal wash-house; later, there were very many in Glasgow
'Talk of the steamie' = topic of gossip

All good things...

When it came to food and shelter, there were eating houses, taverns, inns and lodgings, as well as the coffee shops. And also fleshers (butchers), salt-fish merchants, bakers, pastry-makers, confectioners, a gingerbread-maker(!), grocers, greengrocers, tea merchants, tobacconists, maltsters (malt-makers), brewers, vintners (winemakers), distillers and a great many spirit sellers. (Too many: one shop selling alcohol for every 14 households, it was said. From 1828, the city authorities tried to limit them.)

If over-consumption made Glaswegians feel ill, they might consult a chemist, druggist or 'seller of patent medicines'. When business was going badly, they might need to use a pawnbroker, or try to reclaim debts through Glasgow's small-claims court, which met almost every day.

Down by the river, there were victuallers: men and women who sold provisions to ships' quartermasters preparing for long voyages. There were mills to grind flour, and granaries to store grain. Right in the middle of the city, there were cow-keepers, too. Without refrigerators to store milk, Glasgow's dairymen and maids needed fresh milk to sell every day. There were also meal (oats and barley) and hay sellers, and livery stables, where horses could be hired.

Shops, eating houses and taverns stood next to professional people's offices. By the 1830s, Glasgow had lawyers, accountants, bankers, publishers, booksellers and printers, journalists, schoolmasters, music teachers, tax collectors, insurance brokers and agents, land surveyors, engineers, architects, auctioneers, university lecturers, clergymen, midwives and a freelance professor of French.

Professionals, merchants and prosperous craftworkers and traders all kept live-in servants and hired extra help by the day. There were also, by 1830, over 100,000 men and women working in industry, either at home as outworkers, or in factories. Down by the docks, there were sailors and dockers and porters and warehousemen and ferrymen. (And places for them all to eat, drink and sleep.) Throughout Glasgow, there were builders, wrights (woodworkers), slaters, glaziers, plasterers, pottery makers, blacksmiths and ironworkers, oil and coal merchants, candle makers and sellers, carters and carriers. Rag collectors collected rubbish for recycling; scavengers, under the control of the city police, tried to keep the streets clean.

Perhaps most intriguing of all were the specialist craft-workers, who made tools and instruments needed by other skilled artisans, or luxurious, fashionable items for Glasgow's wealthiest households. For example, in directories we can find marble cutters, pattern makers, gunmakers, lithographers, engravers, china and glass sellers, piano sellers, musical instrument makers, typefounders, an umbrella maker, a seal engraver, a clock-face maker, an oil and colour dealer (for paints), a gold-ornament maker and a japanner (person who decorated items with lacquer). And an 'importer of fancy articles', plus the proprietor of an 'Italian warehouse', who sold goods from Mediterranean lands.

'Business and bustle'

'We then walked a considerable time in the streets, which are perhaps as handsome as streets can be... The Trongate, an old street, is very picturesque – high houses, with an intermixture of gable fronts towards the street. The New Town is built of fine stone, in the best style of the very best London streets at the west end of the town, but, not being of brick, they are greatly superior. One thing must strike every stranger in his first walk through Glasgow – an appearance of business and bustle, but no coaches or gentlemen's carriages... I also could not but observe a want of cleanliness in the appearance of the lower orders of the people, and a dullness in the dress and outside of the whole mass, as they moved along...'

Recollections of a Tour Made in Scotland,
Dorothy Wordsworth, 1803

Women mean business

As Glasgow statistician James Cleland observed, looking back from the early 1800s, '...the ladies of these days did not think it beneath them to ply the needle, nurture their own children, to make their own markets or to superintend the cooking of their husbands' dinners...'

There were also many successful and (sometimes) wealthy businesswomen. Here are just a few of them – taken, as a random sample, from those listed under the letter 'B' in *Pigot and Co's Commercial Directory of 1837*:

Bain Isabella & Agnes, smallware [cutlery etc] dealers, 234 Argyle St
Ballantyne Isabel, victualler, 74 King St, Tradeston
Ballantyne Miss, lodgings, 41 North Albion St
Bannatyne Margaret, dress maker, 145 Main street, Anderston
Bannerman Margaret, straw hat maker, 184 West Nile St
Barclay Jane, cow keeper, 17 Nelson St
Barland Agnes, milliner, 30 Hope St
Barbour Janet, bleacher, Woodside, Chapelfield
Barr Agnes, druggist, 61 Main St
Barrett Margaret, victual dealer, Broomielaw

Barrie Mary, victualler, 132 Campbell St
Barton Mrs. lodgings, Adaras' Court,
  Argyle St
Beggs Mrs. lodgings, 74 Argyle St
Bell Agnes, milliner 132 Sanchyhall [sic] St
Bell Ann, dress maker, 1 Oxford St
Bell Charlotte, milliner, 97 Kirk St, Tradeston
Bell Mrs. lodgings, 52 Glassford St
Bisket Mrs. milliner, 44 Bell St
Bissett Mrs. A. dress maker, 10 Stockwell Place
Black Mary, greengrocer, 103 George St
Black Sarah, spirit dealer, 24 Blackfriars
Blackburn Jane, spirit dealer, 94 Eglinton
Blair Mrs. A. lodgings, Adam's Ct, Argyle St
Blair Elizabeth, lodgings, 175 Buchanan St
Blair Janet, eating house, 255 Argyle St
Blythe Jean, spirit dealer, 30 East Clyde St
Bogle Isabella, spirit dealer, Main st, Bridgeton
Bolton Jane, confectioner, 79 Glassford St
Broom Miss, lodgings, Pratt's Court
Bowman Elizabeth, ladies' shoemaker, 160
  Trongate
Brown Margaret, victualler, 9 Melville St
Bowman Helen, stay maker, 23 East Clyde St
Brown Mary, baker, 88 High St
Brough Ann, lodgings, 60 Gordon St
Brown Agnes, furnisher, 6 Eglinton St
Brown Agnes, spirit dealer, 4 St Ninian St
Bowes Euphemia, flesher, 16 Mutton Market

from the cradle to the grave

If we could follow just one typical Glasgow citizen, from a moderately prosperous family, all through his life, what opportunities and experiences would his home town give him? Let's make a little list.

- Birth: Almost certainly at home. Tended by male doctors or professional female midwives if the family was rich; by local wise woman or older female family members if poor. Followed by baptism in one of Glasgow's many churches (some new, some old) belonging to several different branches of the Christian faith, including small groups of Nonconformists. (Church attendance was officially compulsory, though, in big towns, most poor people did not obey the rules.) Glaswegians spoke Scots, and so personal names were traditional and very similar to English ones. Surnames might, however, be Scots/English versions of Highland Gaelic names.

- Schooling: By around 1800, there were 114 schools in Glasgow, with 17,000 pupils attending, girls as well as boys. Many schools were run by religious organisations or charities; around one-third of all pupils got free places or help with the fees.

- College: If our example citizen was intelligent, and his parents could pay the fairly modest fees, he could receive some of the best and most advanced teaching in Europe. The university, now in splendid buildings in the High Street, continued to encourage rational, logical thinking and scientific study. From 1796, there was a second higher education college in Glasgow: Anderson's Institution, which focused on applied science, engineering and technology, and a private medical college.

- Alternative training: If our young man came from a merchant family, he might follow older relatives into the business. If he showed manual, engineering or artistic skills, he might seek an apprenticeship to become an expert craftworker or new-style engineer. If he were mechanically minded and ambitious, he might hope to train 'on the job' as a factory overseer. Or he might work in a shop, or an office, or in the food industry. Or join the army, or go to sea.

- Rest and recreation: Glasgow had two main theatres: the Theatre Royal, opened 1867, now the oldest surviving theatre in Scotland. The Caledonian was less prestigious but very popular. If he liked dancing and could afford a ticket to enter, he might go to the Assembly

Rooms. A reader? Then Glasgow's first circulating library opened in 1783, and there were four by 1800, plus one subscription library. Glasgow also had Scotland's first public library; it opened in 1804, complete with a children's section. With radical ideas? Then he might join one of several reading societies, to discuss them. Poor but keen to learn? Then by 1830, Glasgow had three Mechanics' Institutes. The Hunterian Museum, at the university, was full of weird and wonderful anatomical specimens, collected by 'founder of scientific surgery', John Hunter. There was also a little privately run museum at Glasgow Zoo.

- Sport for all? Not quite, but there were bowls and golf and archery and army marching exercises on Glasgow Green, and prize-fights and cockfights as well. Football was popular among Irish migrants to Glasgow. Horse racing was a particular Glaswegian favourite; over 100,000 spectators flocked to the racecourse in nearby Paisley.

- Sickness and health: With luck, if our typical Glaswegian fell ill he'd be nursed back to health by a family member. The standard medicine was whisky (cheap and rough) or more expensive and palatable brandy. There were chemists (pharmacists) to consult in their shops. There were several hospitals in Glasgow by around 1800 (see page 128) but few patients went there willingly. Only the very rich could afford private surgeons, physicians and nurses.

- Death and burial: Glasgow's population increase meant that old burial grounds were getting full. And so a new cemetery was planned (although not formally opened until 1833). The Necropolis (city of the dead, for Glasgow's wealthy) was laid out on a rocky slope close to the cathedral – strange to say, on the site that eccentric archaeologist Ludovic Mann (see page 128) later claimed to be a temple honouring the prehistoric Moon-goddess. In fact, since 1825 the Necropolis has been dominated by a column 17.5 m high topped with a statue of Scottish Protestant reformer John Knox – who was about as far from being a Moon-worshipper as could be imagined. However, before then, all Glasgow burial grounds were troubled by graverobbers. Like Edinburgh's Burke and Hare, they dug up bodies to sell them to professors of anatomy. After a sensational trial of a grave robber in 1814 (he was acquitted), many Glasgow graves were fitted with mortsafes (locked iron-bar 'cages').

Enter at own risk!

Glaswegians from poor families had little to fall back on if they lost their jobs or became ill. Poverty led to malnutrition. Overcrowding led to dirty and insanitary conditions; there was not enough clean drinking water and no effective sewage system. Disease was rife and there were many accidents. The stresses and strains of everyday life could cause, or exacerbate, mental-health problems.

Wealthy, well-meaning Glaswegians gave money to build and run charitable institutions to care for their most unfortunate fellow citizens. They meant well – though they also wanted to 'cleanse' their own surroundings. Even so, entering Glasgow's hospitals was a last resort for poor and suffering people. Many patients went there to die.

With apologies, the original names for these institutions are used here. Of course we would not use such names today.

- **Royal Infirmary (still there, in newer buildings): Had an isolation ward for fevers, plus 'a laboratory, an apothecary's shop, hot and cold baths, and strong chambers for the temporary restraint of the insane'.**

- Deaf and Dumb Asylum: If people could not communicate, they could not work. They were poor and often outcast from everyday society.

- Lunatic Asylum: Built to the latest 19th-century designs, with wards surrounding a central observation post, to allow superintendents (not quite prison warders, not quite nurses) to keep an eye on all the patients, all the time.

- Asylum for the Blind: The staff who ran this seem genuinely to have tried to help their patients, though – with the benefit of hindsight – it seems that they might also have been using them as guinea pigs, to further their own scientific interests or careers.

- Magdalen Asylum: A home for women who had been sex-workers and/or had given birth out of wedlock; often they had been abused or betrayed. Its supporters hoped to 'reform' the residents as well as care for them.

- Lock Hospital: A place where women with sexually transmitted infections were locked away to stop them passing on their illnesses. (In the 19th century, diseases of this kind were almost always seen as the woman's fault.) They almost all died.

- Hutcheson's Hospital: Founded by lawyer brothers to provide care and pensions for aged men and women.

- St Nicholas Hospital: A medieval almshouse; a care home for 12 aged men.

- The Town Hospital: The dreaded poorhouse, where desperately poor men and women sought food and shelter. Inmates with illness or disability were cared for in one part of the building; the 'able poor' were made to work in another.

- Female Orphan Institution: Gave food and shelter to girls – often foundlings (abandoned babies) – without any other means of support. Perhaps complicit in child abuse (see opposite).

- Eye Infirmary: Where pioneering surgeons and physicians tried to cure eye injuries and diseases.

- There were also many small, private charities – including Church-run organisations – that gave money to support aged people in their own homes. Some also provided food or clothing for cold and hungry factory children. You had to be very, very poor to receive help, and there was not enough of it to go around.

'A fate worse than Death'

In 2002, Glasgow researcher Anna Forrest revealed the appalling secrets of 'The Lock'. Not only were sick women subjected to dangerous and disgusting treatments, but several of the inmates were children, mostly orphans and foundlings. Forrest suggested that these young girls had caught deadly diseases as a result of being sold as 'cures' to older men. (In the past, it was believed that sleeping with a virgin would cure many maladies.)

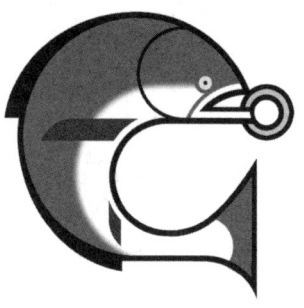

> **6** Second city of
> the Empire **9**

Popular nineteenth-century
description of Glasgow

> **6** The poorer classes of
> Glasgow excel even
> those of Liverpool in the
> bad eminence of filth,
> uncombed and unwashed
> children, disorderly
> deportment, evil smell
> and all that makes city-
> poverty disgusting **9**

American novelist and traveller,
Nathaniel Hawthorne, 1853

CHAPTER FIVE

WORKSHOP OF THE WORLD

In the 1870s, it was a common sight to see one or two fat pigs being trotted through the streets of Glasgow on leads, with decorative ribbons tied to their tails. What were they doing? Advertising grocery shops run by go-getting grocer Thomas Lipton! Clearly the bold commercial spirit that had helped Glasgow tobacco and sugar barons prosper had not left the city. But in the 19th century, it was new mass production and heavy industry, rather than commerce, that made Glasgow grow even greater. Other sights in Glasgow streets included giant ladles full of white-hot molten steel trundling from melting shops to casting shops, and massive steam locomotives (railway vehicles) being hauled from factories to be loaded on ships at Glasgow docks.

In 1836, John M'Ure alias Campbel (his publisher's spellings) expressed a feeling that must surely seem familiar to anyone attempting to write about Glasgow's past. In a preface to his splendidly titled *Glasghu Facies: A View of the City of Glasgow; Or, An Account of Its Origin, Rise, and Progress, with a more Particular description thereof than has hitherto been known*, he both apologises and explains: 'To describe all things in this City, worthy to be known, would take up a large Volume.'

Readers, I know just what M'Ure/ Campbel meant, as this is a very small book. Furthermore, an awful lot of water has flowed under Glasgow's bridges since the 1830s, and there are plenty more bridges, too (20, at the last count). Glasgow in the 19th century was a phenomenal place; a place that changed the world. With limited space, it's not easy to do justice to the city, its people and their achievements.

Even so, let's make a start. What made 19th-century Glasgow richer and bigger – and better and worse – than it had been around 100 years before? Here's a little list:

Industry, Technology, Population, Transport and Trade. There was also a new, proactive attitude towards city living standards by local leaders, and, of course, the well-established enterprising Glasgow spirit. Taken one by one, Glasgow's 19th century developments in any of these areas would have been remarkable. But by synergy – interacting with and supporting each other – they made Glasgow a world-beater.

Steaming ahead

Already, in the late 18th century, Glasgow was a centre of mass textile production; the leading linen-manufacturing city in Scotland. But most of this work, spinning and weaving, took place at home, using hand- (and foot-) powered machines. By 1851, over 37,000 people in Glasgow – one-tenth of the city's population – were involved in cotton cloth manufacture: spinning, weaving, bleaching, dyeing and printing. All those processes were now carried out using steam-powered machines; some used Glasgow factory-made chemicals, as well.

'All is the gift of industry'*

As well as cotton, Glasgow factories also used steam power to produce carpets, chemicals, soap, glass, paper, leather – used for workers' boots and driving belts on machines – and vast quantities of iron. This was produced in Glasgow foundries from ore and coal quarried and mined nearby, and carried to the city by canal and, later, by railways.

Machine-made

In 1865, the American-based Singer Corporation chose 'mechanised' Glasgow as the site of its first overseas factory. Singer's sewing machines enabled clothes and household furnishings to be produced much more cheaply, in factories or at home. By around 1910, Singer's works – moved to Clydebank – covered 40 hectares, employed over 14,000 men and women, turned out 1.3 million machines every year and had its own railway station.

* Scottish poet James Thomson, 'Autumn', 1730

Iron trades – shipbuilding, toolmaking, heavy engineering, armaments and machine components, architectural castings, massive iron beams for buildings, and locomotive construction – overtook textiles as Glasgow's main manufactures during the second half of the 19th century. Parkhead Forge at the east end of Glasgow also pioneered large steel castings and armoured steel plate-making.

'Draw thy fierce streams of blinding ore,
Smite on a thousand anvils, roar
Down to the harbour-bars;
Smoulder in smoky sunsets, flare
On rainy night, with street and square
Lie empty to the stars.
From terrace proud to alley base
I know thee as my mother's face.'

Glasgow-born Alexander Smith, 1857

Industry and trade: Glasgow makes (and sells) it!

1786 Clyde Ironworks opens at Tollcross in Glasgow; it uses iron ore and coal from the Glasgow region.

1776 Adam Smith publishes *An Inquiry Into The Nature and Causes of the Wealth of Nations*. The start of modern economic thinking.

1800 Charles Tennant sets up factory to produce chemicals for industry; by 1900 it becomes the largest in the world.

1800-1830 Iron foundries in Glasgow and along the Clyde import iron from elsewhere in Scotland to make machine parts, nails and iron frames for factory buildings.

1805 Colliery at Govan has expanded. Now employs over 130 men.

1815 Glasgow engineers begin to design and make machines for export to the colonies.

1820 New industrial whisky distilleries built at Port Dundas, in Glasgow.

1821 David Napier opens factory at Lancefield to build ships' engines; Glasgow shipbuilding industry grows fast.

1828 James Neilson's Hot Blast furnace makes iron-smelting cheaper and quicker. The new furnaces use blackband ore, mined near Glasgow. Iron-making in Glasgow develops rapidly.

1830 Robert Napier sets up large shipyard at Govan on south bank of Clyde; ships are fitted with his new steam boilers.

1830 There are now 107 mills spinning cotton in Glasgow and its suburbs.

1837 Parkhead Forge opens. At its busiest, around 1910, it employs 40,000 workers.

1844 Glasgow Stock Exchange opens. Many Glasgow engineering and manufacturing companies are owned by shareholders, not by old-style merchants and their families.

1861 American Civil War disrupts supplies of raw cotton; Glasgow cotton industry declines.

1864 Now more than 20 shipyards on the Clyde.

1867–1912 Six new deep-water docks opened on the Clyde at Glasgow, with huge cranes and other facilities for handling bulk import/export cargoes.

1874 Glasgow produces over half the UK's new ships.

1880s Further improvements to steam-engine design (triple expansion) mean that Glasgow shipping companies now dominate sea routes to Canada, South America, Africa, India and East Asia.

1903 Engineering companies merge to form North British Locomotive Company. It employs over 8,000 workers and makes locomotives for railways all over the world.

1914 By now, there are 17.7 km (11 miles) of docks in Glasgow and downriver on either side of the Clyde.

1914 River Clyde at Clydebank now 10 metres deep. Glasgow is UK's third most important port, after London and Liverpool.

food for mind and body

Other industries soon developed to feed Glasgow's growing population and to meet the needs of people living throughout the west of Scotland. Brewing (Tennent's, for centuries), baking, distilling and soft-drink making (Irn-Bru, 1901), papermaking, book printing and binding (Collins, 1819), newspaper printing (*Glasgow Herald*, from 1783), confectionery (Tunnock's, 1890) and many, many more.

In and out

Goods made in Glasgow were exported all round the world from Glasgow's new deep-water harbour. As well as narrowing and scouring a shipping channel for larger-size ships, from the 1850s to the 1880s Glasgow engineers also dredged millions of tonnes of silt and gravel from the river bottom. Once this gargantuan task was completed, the largest ocean-going ships could sail right to the heart of Glasgow. They carried imported coal and raw materials for Glasgow factories, together with imported grain, frozen meat – from as far away as Argentina – and fruit, to

Transport

1790 Forth and Clyde canal completed.

1793 Monkland Canal completed.

1802 The world's first practical steam-powered boat, *Charlotte Dundas*, pulls barges on Forth and Clyde canal.

1803 First-known racing yacht built on the Clyde.

1812 First commercial steam-powered ship, *PS Comet*, launched on the Clyde. Engines made in Glasgow, hull built in Port Glasgow.

1814 Now nine steam boats on the Clyde.

1818 First shipyard opens at Glasgow.

1826–1831 First steam-powered Scottish locomotives made in Glasgow for Monkland and Kirkintilloch Railway.

1831 Glasgow Railway opens, to carry coal.

1840s 'Railway mania'; Glasgow–Edinburgh railway built; railways link Glasgow to Dundee, Aberdeen, south-west Scotland and England.

1840s Production of iron-hulled passenger ships starts in Glasgow.

1842 Queen Street Station built.

1845 Horse-drawn omnibuses in Glasgow.

1849 Buchanan Street Station built.

1872 First tram rails laid; tramcars are pulled by horses.

1879 Central Station built.

1880s Fastest rail journey London to Glasgow now only 8 hours.

1890 River Clyde dredging means that ships of 7.5 metres draught can now sail up to Glasgow.

1896 Glasgow Subway opens.

1898–1902 First electric trams in Glasgow.

Science and technology: pure Glasgow genius

1769 James Watt (maker of mathematical instruments at University of Glasgow) patents improved steam-engine design; it is much more efficient and potentially much more powerful.

1772 American electrical experimenter Benjamin Franklin installs pioneering lightning conductor on Glasgow Cathedral spire.

1792 First steam-powered cotton-spinning mill in Glasgow.

1797 Charles Tennant invents new process for chemically bleaching cloth.

1800 First steam pump at Glasgow breweries.

c1810 First steam-powered cotton weaving loom in Glasgow.

1818 Public (coal) gas supply begins in Glasgow.

1823 Charles Macintosh invents waterproof cloth in Glasgow.

1828 James Neilson invents the hot-blast furnace process, at Glasgow Gasworks.

1830 Robert Napier invents more efficient and cheaper steam boiler to power ships.

1842 Glasgow Botanic Gardens opens; promotes scientific study of plants.

1848 Glasgow Professor William Thomson (later Lord Kelvin) develops absolute temperature scale; it is later named after him.

1855 Physicist Macquorn Rankine becomes professor at University of Glasgow. He campaigns to apply science to industry, writes textbooks and introduces the first theory-plus-practice 'sandwich' courses to train engineers.

1865 Joseph Lister pioneers antiseptic surgery at Glasgow Royal Infirmary – after fainting at the smell of patients' rotting flesh.

1865–1913 Sewing-machine technology revolutionises the production of clothes and furnishings.

1875 Sir William Macewen pioneers surgery techniques at Glasgow Royal Infirmary. Also encourages professional nurse training.

All gone

In the past, just like today, there was often an environmental cost to development. Industrial districts of Glasgow, and the River Clyde itself, became horribly polluted.

'Where is now the River purer than amber, and the "siller [silver] Salmon" that were wont to sport in its Shallows and Pools? The Salmon are gone, but the River still remains, and has become a Sink and Receptacle of every abomination generated in the midst of a vast Population. The Gardens, the Orchards, and the green Fields… are also gone. The stately Mansions have either been demolished or are turned into Whisky Shops, Ham-Stores, Old-Clothes Emporiums, Brokers'-Stalls, and common Lodging-Houses…'

The Note Book of a Native, Glasgow Weekly Herald, *1869.*

feed Glasgow citizens. The quantities were staggering: by 1911 Glasgow imports and exports totalled almost 10 million tonnes. Little 'puffers' (coastal steamships) also sailed from Glasgow, distributing Glasgow manufactures and imported goods to England and Ireland, as well as the west coast of Scotland.

Applied science

None of Glasgow's industrial revolutions could have happened without inventions and discoveries made by Glasgow's leading scientists and engineers. Unlike 'ivory tower' academics elsewhere, Glasgow's professors were keen to work closely with businessmen and inventors from the tough and dirty real-life industrial world. And, just as importantly, many Glasgow factory owners and shipbuilders were willing to contribute their own knowledge and experience, as well as to learn from the latest academic discoveries.

'High skilled, low paid'

As today's Glasgow City Council slogan proudly proclaims, 'People Make Glasgow'. That's true right now, and possibly was even more true of Glasgow in the 19th century. None of the city's industries or businesses would have been able to prosper or expand without a good – in every way – source of labour. Many workers were highly skilled, though their wages were usually miserable. Creating fine fabrics (Glasgow's cottons were top-end), dealing with molten metals or deadly chemicals, or constructing ships or bridges or railways where a mistake could cost hundreds of lives took aptitude, training, hard work and dedication. Where did all those people come from?

A home from home?

'We have Lodging-Houses kept by the O'Donghertys, the Trainers, and Widow Carroll ; there is the "London-derry" Hotel for the Orangemen, and the " Emerald Isle" Tavern for the Papists*; Spirit-Cellars are kept by the Kellys, the Conaghans, and the Macnamees; Washing and Dressing is done by Mrs. Harkin; and a Bag-Store is kept by O'Connor...

At the South-Eastern extremity of the Street... we noticed an old House... the under Floor is now composed of Shops, one of them occupied by Mr. Arthur Finnigan, who deals in second-hand Watches, Jewellery, Gems, and Musical Instruments. The upper Story is occupied by Mr. James Lynch, as an Undertaker's Establishment; and he, at the same time, lets out Coaches, Gigs, Hearses...'

History of Glasgow from the earliest to the present times by Writers of Eminence, *edited and published by John Tweed, Glasgow, 1873*

* Roman Catholics; today this word is considered offensive and should not be used.

Firstly, from around Scotland. Times were tough in the Highlands and Islands; Glasgow was the obvious place for poor families to move to. Even today, many Glaswegians identify with and maintain links to ancestral districts all over the west of Scotland. Secondly, from Ireland. It's barely 160 km from Glasgow to Ireland's coast. Even before the potato famine of the 1840s, Irish people were coming to Glasgow, often just for a few months at a time, to earn money before returning home.

After the famine, migration from Ireland increased. Between 1841 and 1851, the number of Irish living in Glasgow almost doubled. Irish men found work as labourers, in the docks or in heavy industries. Irish women worked in cotton mills or as household servants and cleaners. Some ran lodging houses for Irish labourers. Once in Glasgow, Irish families stayed close to each other in poor districts of the city, where rents were cheaper. They also tended to marry other Irish migrants. About three-quarters of the Irish people who came to live in Glasgow were Roman Catholic; the pre-existing tensions between Irish Catholics and Protestants were continued in the city.

A new home

In the late 19th century, new groups of migrants came to Glasgow, seeking work or freedom from persecution. Italians set up successful food shops and restaurants. German, Scandinavian and Baltic sailors worked on ships in the Clyde. There were German businessmen, as well, and two German-speaking church congregations. Jewish people, from Russia, the Baltic and eastern Europe first came to Glasgow in 1823; they settled in the Gorbals district and in Garnethill. By 1880, there were over 800 members of the synagogue there. Groups of Roma people, also from eastern Europe, were allowed to settle in Glasgow after being refused permission in Edinburgh. However, they were allocated living space in one of Glasgow's most polluted industrial districts: Vinegarhill.

Hell on earth?

Many newcomers prospered, but, especially to begin with, migrants arriving in Glasgow joined the poorest city residents who were already living in unspeakably awful slums. In crumbling cottages and tall tenements

Glasgow's Shame

'In the very centre of the city there is an accumulated mass of squalid wretchedness which is probably unequalled in any other town of the British dominions.'

Chief Constable of Glasgow, 1840.

Translated into individual misery, that meant:

'...the Green [next to the Saltmarket] is all alive with squalid Groups... Beguiled by the radiance of the Summer noon, they have sneaked forth, for a brief interval... Unfortunate Females, with faces of triple brass hiding hearts of unutterable woe, sleeping Girls, who might be mistaken for lifeless bundles of Rags, – dim-looking Scoundrels, with Felony stamped on every feature, – owlish-looking Knaves, skulking half-ashamed at their own appearance in the eye of day... [and] poor little tattered and hungry-looking Children, with precocious lines of care upon their old-mannish features, tumble about on the brown and sapless Herbage...

Glasghu facies: a view of the city of Glasgow; or, An account of its origin [&c.] by J. M'Ure.

(apartment blocks) surviving from earlier centuries, whole families were crowded into a single damp, draughty room, with no heating, clean water or sanitation. Killer diseases spread rapidly: measles, cholera, typhus, TB. In 1820, the average age of death in Glasgow was 42 for a man and 45 for a woman; this fell still lower as industrial pollution, smoke from coal fires, malnutrition and disabilities caused by accidents at work made life even more precarious. Although Glasgow city leaders tried hard to improve housing stock and living conditions, at the end of the 19th century Glasgow was still Britain's most crowded city, and one in seven Glasgow babies died – mostly from diseases that would be treatable today.

Taking action

Clearly, something had to be done. In 1866 Glasgow police introduced 'ticketing' (licensing by inspectors) to check and limit the number of people in each building. Around the same time, the City Council appointed its first medical officer, tasked with improving public health, and began a programme of slum clearances. Charities redoubled their efforts. Queen Victoria herself opened a new scheme that supplied Glasgow with clean water from Loch Katrine near Stirling in 1859. Between 1866 and 1902, 35 hectares of slum buildings were demolished and replaced by 39 new streets, with improvements made to 12 more. New houses – many of them Glasgow's typical tenements – date from this time, but often only the best-paid factory workers could afford to live in them. Even so, large areas of Glasgow remained pretty grim.

'Mrs Barbour's army'

But, 'cometh the hour, cometh the man' – or in Glasgow's case, the women. And pretty formidable they were, too. Ever since 1885, campaigners in Glasgow had been calling for more and better homes for ordinary families. By 1911, there was a crisis. A new law, aiming to help poorer people, allowed rents to be paid monthly rather than yearly in advance. In response, landlords increased rents, and Glasgow tenants protested.

In 1915, the Glasgow Women's Housing Association, led by minister's wife Mary Barbour, together with welfare campaigners Helen Crawfurd, Mary Laird and Jessie Stephen, led a rent strike. Wives, mothers and girls marched in mass demonstrations, and attacked police and factors (agents) who came to evict them – it was said, by pulling down the men's trousers. By the end of 1915, Glasgow trade unions threatened to strike, as well. City and national governments intervened, and rents were frozen.

People

1780 Glasgow population 60,000.

1787 Muslin weavers riot over pay cuts.

1790s Radical Thomas Muir calls for a republic; he is transported.

1800 Food riots by weavers in Calton.

1800 City of Glasgow Police founded; one of the first city police forces in the world.

1801 Glasgow population 77,000.

1806 First (private) scheme to supply water to Glasgow.

1809 General Association of Operative Weavers founded (a Trade Union).

1811 Glasgow now Scotland's biggest city, and second largest in the UK.

1816 Mass meeting on Glasgow Green demands better representation in Parliament, and lower price of bread.

1816 Soup kitchen set up to feed low-paid weavers.

1818 Deadly typhus epidemic.

1820 Radical War: calls for a general strike and rebellion by workers. March from Glasgow towards Carron foundry near Falkirk. Workers' leader James Wilson is hanged.

1821 Glasgow population 147,000.

1830 Around 30 percent of Glasgow-area weavers now of Irish origin.

1831 Glasgow City Corporation sets up Board of Health to fight against disease in the city and to improve sanitation

1832 First-ever Glasgow MP in UK Parliament.

1832 Cholera epidemic; 660 die.

1833 Male cotton-workers at Calton strike to protest against women spinners; they believe women are taking men's jobs.

1835 Now 12 Orange Order Lodges (Irish Protestant groups) in Glasgow.

1837 Cotton-spinners strike for shorter working hours; leaders transported.

1837-1847 Repeated outbreaks of typhus.

1841-1848 Chartist campaigns and demonstrations call for the right to vote, reform of Parliament and an end to corruption in politics.

1845 Scottish Poor Law Act provides basic help for the sick and starving. Poverty and living conditions in Glasgow city slums still grim.

1846 Burgh boundaries moved; Glasgow doubles in size as a result.

1848-1849 Cholera kills around 4,000 in Glasgow.

1851 Glasgow population now almost 360,000; 16% born in Ireland.

1854 Cholera kills 3,800 in Glasgow.

1858 Trades Council formed to unite and strengthen small Glasgow trade unions and plan collective action.

1859 Queen Victoria opens Glasgow's new clean water supply, from Loch Katrine.

1862 Glasgow appoints first City Medical Officer to improve public health; first Free Hospital founded, to care for Glasgow poor.

1866 City Improvement Trust starts to clear Glasgow's worst slums.

1867 Child labour (under 8) now illegal; by law, children aged 8–13 can only work part-time.

1870s Demand for more labour increases industrial wages in Glasgow.

1872 Compulsory free elementary (primary) schooling for children.

1877 Mitchell Library (magnificent public library) opens in Glasgow.

1881 Glasgow population: 83% born in Scotland; 13% in Ireland; 3% in England; 1% elsewhere.

1883 The Boys' Brigade founded in Glasgow: the world's first voluntary uniformed youth group. It aims to encourage Christian values, good health and self-improvement.

1885 Royal Commission calls for more housing to be built for Glasgow workers.

1890s City sewers rebuilt.

1890s First socialist city councillors elected in Glasgow to represent working people.

1894 New sewage treatment plant for Glasgow.

1901 Glasgow population now 760,000.

1902 Football now popular among Glasgow workers. Ibrox Disaster: 25 spectators killed and over 500 injured as stand collapses during Scotland–England match.

1906 First Labour Party MP appointed for Glasgow.

1906–1914 Glasgow suffragettes call for Votes for Women; stage violent protests in the city. They are sent to Glasgow gaols.

1911 'Scientific Management' practices introduced at the Singer sewing-machine factory provoke a mass strike.

1915 Glasgow Rent Strike: women refuse to pay rent for squalid, unhealthy homes.

1919 Shameful race riot by Glasgow seamen who fear that Chinese crewmen and black sailors from British colonies will take over their jobs.

1919 Battle of George Square: army tanks and 10,000 troops sent to Glasgow to control mass protests in city centre against unemployment, poverty and lack of workers' rights.

City of contrasts

Reading about Glasgow's poverty and squalor, it's hard to remember that from around 1870, it was one of the wealthiest and most magnificent cities in Europe. Many Glasgow landmarks that are famous today date from around that time – for example, University of Glasgow with its tall tower (1867), the grand City Chambers (1888), Kelvingrove Art Gallery and Museum (completed 1901, and no, it was NOT built the wrong way round, as the Glasgow urban myth insists), the imposing Mitchell Library (1907), and the wonderfully over-the-top Templeton Carpet Factory (1889).

The wide streets and elegant 18th century houses of Glasgow's 'New Town', to the west of the old High Street, were joined by many more impressive residences for wealthy Glasgow shipowners and industrialists, and by pleasant tree-lined avenues and squares for middle-class families. Compared with single-end (one-room) working-class tenements, large, superior tenement apartments might have a cosy parlour, a formal drawing room, a dining room, two or three bedrooms, a small bathroom, a kitchen with a bedroom for a live-in servant, and a cool, hygienic pantry. The close (common access entrance) would often be decorated with glazed 'wally'(ceramic)tiles in glowing colours and elaborate patterns.

Glasgow Style

Glasgow shops now had big, bright plate-glass windows; fine new Glasgow churches were built in styles ranging from ancient Greek to mock-gothic. There were new parks and public gardens, theatres and concert halls, libraries, museums and art galleries, restaurants and genteel tea rooms. It was at around this time in Glasgow that one of the city's best-known sons, architect Charles Rennie Mackintosh, was experimenting with revolutionary new designs. His work is now world famous, especially the elegant art-nouveau Willow Tea Rooms and the recently fire-damaged Glasgow School of Art (completed 1909). Also based in the city, the group of artists known as the Glasgow Boys (and also some Glasgow women) were rebelling against conventional ideas of style and composition. They often painted outdoors, using strong colours to create bright, fresh images. In art, as in industry and technology, Glasgow was ahead of the game.

At the end of the 19th century, crowds, rich and poor, flocked to two magnificent Great Exhibitions, held in 1888 and 1901 in Glasgow's spacious Kelvingrove Park. Visitors were dazzled by international collections of art, machinery, manufactured goods, scientific curiosities, houses, clothes, furniture, foods...

The exhibitions were educational and entertaining. Most important of all, they displayed Glasgow's achievements to itself, to the rest of Scotland and to the world. No wonder the city was proud.

O, beautiful city of Glasgow, which stands on the
river Clyde,
How happy should the people be which in ye reside;
Because it is the most enterprising city of the
present day,
Whatever anybody else may say...

The ships which lie at the Broomielaw are most
beautiful to see,
They are bigger and better than any in Dundee...

Then the warehouses are filled from the floor to
the topmost storey,
With goods which brings Glasgow money
and glory...

O, wonderful city of Glasgow, with your triple
expansion engines,
At the making of which your workmen get
many singeins;
Also the deepening of the Clyde, most marvellous
to behold,
Which cost much money, be it told...

Oh, beautiful city of Glasgow, I must conclude
my lay,
By calling thee the greatest city of the
present day...

From The Beautiful City of Glasgow,
William McGonagall, c 1881

‘ Glasgow's not
just a city, it's an
urban civilisation
in itself. ,

Online blurb for book:
Glasgow: History of a City,
Michael Fry, 2017

CHAPTER SIX

RISE AND FALL?

' ... Happy Glasgow, Clyde's chiefest Pride;
Glory of that and all the world beside...'

Those lines were written almost 400 years ago*. Exaggerated? Yes. Bombastic? Yes. Unrealistic? Yes, that too. But they still set out a pretty good ambition for Glasgow's future.

The years between 1901, when Glasgow's second Great Exhibition was held, and the eve of World War I were in many ways a golden age for Glasgow. In spite of its problems and inequalities, Glasgow did achieve 'glory'. So should we leave our story there, when Glasgow was confident, proud and prosperous? After all, some might say that it's been downhill all the way ever since.

* By Arthur Johnston, who died in 1641.

But really, is that fair? Glasgow has certainly lived through long years of slump and depression, but it's also worked very hard at restoring – or recreating – itself. So perhaps it might be more accurate to say that Glasgow's risen, then fallen, and is now on the rise again. How did this happen?

War effort

During World War I, Glasgow was a major centre of armaments and warship production. There was great pressure to produce materiel – 100,000 men worked in shipbuilding alone – and this led to a short-term boost for the economy. Women made munitions and took over other traditionally male jobs, such as driving trams. But trade unions protested at the use of unskilled labour, fearing wage cuts. Around 200,000 Glasgow men served in the armed forces. Over 18,000 died and many more were injured. Few families or neighbourhoods escaped trauma.

A few local heroes

• Walter Tull

Adopted by a Glasgow family, Tull excelled at sport. He played for Spurs and Northampton and was the first black player signed by Glasgow Rangers F.C. He served as an officer in the British army and died in action in 1918.

• Cleweth Donaldson

Son of a Glasgow shipping magnate, he joined the newly formed Royal Flying Corps. Flying on an extremely risky reconnaissance mission, he was shot down and killed in 1917.

• Dr Louise McIlroy

Glasgow doctor, specialising in the care of women and babies. But in wartime, she went to the Front to manage field hospitals treating wounded soldiers in France and eastern Europe. She saved hundreds of lives, in difficult and dangerous conditions.

And there were so many more.

fears for the future

After World War I ended, there was a world-wide depression in trade, which deepened after the Wall Street Crash of 1929. Fewer ships were ordered from Glasgow yards, fewer machines and tools were manufactured and less steel was made. There was no need for so many dockers, drivers, miners and foundry workers, and much less money to spend in shops and public houses. Jobs for working men and women were hard to find; by the early 1930s, one in three of the Glasgow workforce was unemployed.

from bad to worse

Unemployment worsened the poverty already suffered by many Glaswegians. In the 1920s and 1930s, many thousands of families could only afford crumbling, crowded lodgings in Glasgow slums. The Gorbals district, south of the Clyde, became a byword for degradation. As late as 1957, over 90% of the housing there had 'inadequate' sanitation. Some reports were sensationalised, but – at a time before the Welfare State – the suffering was genuine.

Red Clydeside

Militant political action was well-known in Glasgow. There had been the Rent Strike (see pages 155 and 159) and, from 1909–1914 Glasgow suffragettes had staged many violent protests, including planting bombs in the Botanic Gardens. Between 1914–1918, there were marches by anti-war campaigners. In 1919, a mass demonstration by around 90,000 Glasgow workers led to bloody clashes between police and protesters in Glasgow's George Square.

What did rioters want? Shorter working hours, better working conditions and job security. Over 60,000 new residents had come to live in Glasgow between 1912 and 1915. In wartime, they had found work, but now what would they do? The UK government in London feared that a socialist uprising was beginning; some protesters were waving a red flag, the sign of revolution. It sent tanks and armed soldiers.

In the UK General Election of 1922, Labour Party candidates, who supported the workers, were elected as 10 out of Glasgow's 15 MPs.

All the industrial areas of Glasgow were very unhealthy; the air was filled with smoke and fumes, and streams and ditches ran green with waste and chemical pollution. Glasgow's blonde and russet sandstone terraces were coated with black soot. Tuberculosis and rickets (a bone disease caused by lack of vitamin D) were rife. Glasgow citizens had the lowest life expectancy of anywhere in Britain.

The Jeely Piece Club

In spite of tough circumstances and dismal prospects, many Glasgow men, women and children have worked hard to improve the lives of their fellow citizens. The Jeely Piece Club is one of the city's most famous self-help projects. It was founded in the 1970s at Castlemilk, a new, overcrowded, crime-ridden, high-rise council housing scheme, by local women including church minister's wife, Mary Miller. It provided play and learning opportunities for children and friendship and support for their parents, helping to create a stronger and safer community in very difficult conditions.

Weegie words

'The accent of the lowest state of Glaswegians is the ugliest one can encounter.'* Beauty is in the eye of the beholder, but Glasgow's language has historic interest – even if it's not always easy for outsiders to comprehend.

Early inhabitants of Glasgow spoke Brythonic. In the Middle Ages, this was replaced by Scots (a language related to English), although visitors from the north and west would have spoken Gaelic. Churchmen and council officials wrote in Latin; university students studied this too. From around 1700, refined Scottish English was spoken by some wealthy, well-connected Glaswegians, but Scots remained the norm – plus new words learned from foreign trade or overseas migrants. In the 19th and 20th centuries, education and the media introduced standard English. But many Glaswegians, even today, still 'speak Glasga' as well. Well-known 'weegie words' include:

wee donder = walk
clatty = dirty
swally = alcoholic drink
yaldy = great energy or excitement
glaikit = stupid

* *Mid 20th-century university lecturer.*

Gangland

The poorest areas of Glasgow were terrorised by razor gangs (armed with cut-throat knives). From the late 19th century, gangs had combined violent crime and religious sectarianism (Protestant versus Catholic) in a vicious cocktail. Recruits were mostly unemployed young men who felt hopeless and frustrated. Joining a gang gave them an identity, and they could earn respect from other gang members. Gangs fought each other and the police and bullied, blackmailed and demanded protection money from local businesses. Each gang patrolled its own territory, creating dangerous no-go areas for outsiders. To try to keep control, Glasgow police were said to have searched for tall, strong recruits from the Highlands, free from Glasgow connections, and famously tough and hardy.

Scheming...

In 1912, 1926 and 1930, Glasgow's boundaries were widened to include several nearby suburbs. Greenfield land was also purchased by the city council for new housing schemes:

estates of low-rise flats and small family houses with gardens. By 1938, the city covered an area of 75 square kilometres, and had a population of over one million. But although over 35,000 new council homes had been built, surveys found that almost half of Glasgow's homes were still overcrowded.

Bombs and blackouts

World War II hit Glasgow hard. Its shipyards and factories, now working at full capacity for the war effort, were an obvious target for enemy attack. In the Clydebank Blitz of 1941, a key industrial district was attacked. Over 500 residents were killed, and almost 12,000 buildings were damaged. Bombs fell in many other parts of the city as well, and over 100,000 Glasgow children were evacuated for safety. The River Clyde was guarded by an underwater barricade of sunken ships and tough wire netting, and 'decoy cities' (patterns of lights and timber buildings) were set up outside the city and away from the docks to confuse enemy night bombers. The years after World War II would also bring big changes to Glasgow's buildings.

All fall down

It seemed like a good idea at the time: tear down old slums and build high in the sky. That way, re-homed families could still stay within Glasgow, paying rents and taxes to keep the city running. The first (19-storey) skyscrapers were built in 1953, in the Gorbals, and many more followed. But Glaswegians found that these high-rises did not work; away from their old dirty, crowded but familiar communities – and without the means to go back to them – they felt isolated, depressed and deprived. The new concrete buildings had problems, too. They were hard to maintain and attracted vandals. Old communities were further torn apart when motorways were built through the centre of Glasgow in the 1960s, and when new towns – East Kilbride (1947) and Cumbernauld (1956) – attracted funding for new houses and new jobs for old Glasgow families. As of today, a quarter of Glasgow's post-war high-rises have been demolished.

At the same time, mostly due to changing world trade and cheaper overseas competition, but also to UK government policies, Glasgow's heavy industries were falling into decline. So many skilled workers, so much experience and expertise, all thrown on the scrapheap – or so it seemed. The last great Glasgow-built liner, *Queen Elizabeth II*, was launched in 1969. After years of declining profits and bitter industrial struggles, most of Glasgow's iron and steelworks and shipyards closed in the 1970s.

'Glasgow smiles better!'

But wait, the picture is not all bad. In fact, it's rapidly improving. Since the 1980s, Glasgow city movers and shakers, and Glasgow citizens, have brought about a transformation. It began around 1983, with a rather clunky slogan (above), designed to evoke Glasgow's famous friendliness and hint at fresh possibilities. The same year, a fabulous new art gallery, the Burrell Collection, opened in a park in the south of the city. Rumour has it that the money that financed the collection, amassed by shipping magnate Sir William Burrell (d. 1958), came from insurance gains after he hired 'rust-bucket' ships and sent them – and their sailors – to the bottom of the sea. But that is another story... And it may not be true.

In recent years, Glasgow has become a go-to destination for international events. In 1988, over four million visitors came to see Glasgow's wildly successful Garden Festival; in 1990, Glasgow was European City of Culture; in 1999 it was UK City of Art and Design. In 2002 it was chosen to hold the UEFA Champions' League Final. In 2012, preliminary matches for the 2012 London Olympics were played in Glasgow; in 2014, the Commonwealth Games were held there. They were followed by the European Athletics Championships in 2018.

Glasgow has also overtaken Edinburgh as Scotland's centre for finance and media. Over 18,000 new jobs have been created in a shiny new financial district built on reclaimed industrial land close to the river. Nearby is Glasgow's new digital media quarters, where Scottish radio and TV, and many of Scotland's newspapers, are produced. Glasgow has government and commercial offices and many creative-industry studios. And if you've ever phoned a call centre and heard a Scottish accent, there's a good chance that you've been speaking to someone in Glasgow.

And yet, and yet...

Glasgow is still home to a peculiarly stark set of contrasts: rich and poor; proud and egalitarian; spacious and crowded, all at the same time. There's high culture and high-mindedness; drug and alcohol-fuelled crime and vicious sectarianism. Parts of the city are really beautiful; others undeniably squalid. You can choose from fine food or grotty takeaways; watch super-healthy athletes or come face to face with morbid obesity and / or malnutrition. You can admire world-class architecture or feel depressed by the remaining drab, decaying high-rise flats.

Glasgow's problems have clearly not all gone away. But the city once again offers great opportunities for education, exploration and enjoyment. You can study (at five universities), shoogle (sway) on the squinty bridge, shop till you drop, wonder at the Armadillo (quirky auditorium at the Exhibition Centre), gaze at the Finnieston Crane and the graceful old Tall Ship, or marvel at all the enormous murals. You can rock at the O2 academy, go to bagpipe concerts (yes, really), listen to

Gaelic songs, cheer fierce local football rivals (C'moan Celtic! C'moan Rangers!); watch Glasgow-made movies; enjoy 'a play, a pie and a pint' in a converted church and be intrigued by modern art at the Glue Factory. There are street sculpture and street theatre, plus performances of all kinds in Glasgow parks. Strange but true, if you look up into the trees there, you can see the world's most northerly flock of exotically coloured parakeets. A sign of global warming? Perhaps. But in any case, quite a far cry from St Mungo's robin.

And, almost uniquely in Scotland, you can experience somewhere that's Scottish *and* international. Glasgow has welcomed refugees as well as migrants, and Glaswegians now come from all corners of the globe. Brexit or no Brexit, Glasgow feels European, multicultural and unique, 'an urban civilisation in itself'.

'...and Glasgow belongs to me!'*

Almost everyone's experience of Glasgow is different, because Glasgow is vast and always changing. But from the grandest terraces and the most comfortable suburbs to the grimmest concrete 1950s housing scheme, everyone's a Weegie. Whether they regret the passing of Glasgow's old industrial grandeur or love its new flash and glamour, most wouldn't want to live anywhere else.

In spite of its faults and blemishes, Glasgow still impresses and fascinates visitors, and Glaswegians remain fiercely proud of their city, its great history, its hopeful future, its unique, raw energy – and its remarkable, resilient spirit. 'Let Glasgow Flourish!', indeed.

* *Closing line of 1920s popular song,* 'I belong to Glasgow'.

Glossary

bailie A junior magistrate.

booth A little shop.

burgage plot Division of land in a burgh; a house and outbuildings with a long garden behind.

burgh Town that had the right to run its own local government.

charter Royal or government document, awarding an honour or granting a right.

chroniclers Early historians, who often mixed fiction with facts.

circulating library A library that lends books to members for free.

close Entrance to part of a large tenement building.

coracle Early boat, made of woven reeds or branches covered with leather.

counting house Accounts office.

diocese Unit of Church administration, headed by a bishop.

drumlin Small hill, formed by a glacier.

dubs Puddles or small ponds.

firth River estuary.

fish supper Glaswegian/ Scottish name for fish and chips.

Irn-Bru Sweet, rust-coloured, fizzy soft drink.

Jacobite Supporter of exiled King James VII/II and his descendants, who claimed the right to rule England and Scotland between c 1688 and 1746.

Mechanics' Institute Place of adult education, set up to help working men learn technical subjects.

Nonconformist Christian believer who does not belong to an established church, e.g. the Church of Scotland.

novice A trainee.

Provost / Lord Provost Leader of Glasgow Burgh / City Council.

Radical A person committed to extensive, sometimes revolutionary political and social change.

rational Based on reason and logic.

runes Letters used by early peoples (including Vikings) in the region of Scandinavia.

scheme Glasgow name for council housing estate.

Sectarian Describes rivalry based on religious beliefs (in Glasgow, between Protestants and Catholics).

steamie Communal room for washing clothes and household linens.

subscription library A library used only by members who pay a fee.

vennel (also **wynd**) A narrow lane between houses.

Glasgow timeline

320 million years BC Fossil trees show that Glasgow area was once a hot, steamy swamp.

3 million years BC–12,000 BC Glaciers advance and retreat, and shape the Clyde Valley landscape.

5000 BC Fishing communities on banks of the Clyde.

3000 BC People near Glasgow carve stone monuments.

2700 BC–1400 BC Farmers in the Clyde River valley.

79 BC Romans invade southern Scotland.

AD 142 Romans start to build the Antonine Wall.

c AD 400–800 Glasgow area is ruled from Alt Clut (now Dumbarton Rock) as part of the kingdom of Strathclyde.

c AD 400–800 Govan is an important royal and religious centre.

AD 543 According to legend, St Mungo founds a church and monastery where Glasgow Cathedral now stands.

AD 870 onwards Viking raiders from Dublin attack the kingdom of Strathclyde.

1136 Dedication of new Glasgow Cathedral.

1153 Scots/Norse Lord of the Isles attacks Glasgow.

1175 Glasgow become a burgh (town with legal status and privileges).

1190 Glasgow annual fair given royal charter (license).

1285 First record of a bridge across the Clyde.

1451 The University of Glasgow founded.

1492 Glasgow bishops become archbishops.

1520s onwards Tensions between Roman Catholic archbishops and Protestant reformers.

1546 Glasgow sends first MP to Scottish Parliament.

1560 Scottish Parliament supports Reformation of the Catholic Church. Last Catholic archbishop of Glasgow flees to France.

1567 Mary Queen of Scots visits Glasgow.

1570 Andrew Melville introduces new scientific approach to study at the University of Glasgow.

1579 Protestant reformers plan to demolish Glasgow Cathedral.

1639–1653 Covenanters War; Glasgow supports strict Protestants.

1652 and 1677 Many old Glasgow wooden buildings destroyed by fire.

1660 First Glasgow coal mine, in Gorbals district south of the Clyde.

c 1660–1800 Glasgow developing into 'a city of business'.

1668 New deep-water harbour for Glasgow shipping built at Port Glasgow, downriver on the Clyde.

1670 Glasgow population now around 14,000.

1690 End of bishops' control of Glasgow.

1698–1700 Glasgow merchants lose money in disastrous Darien Scheme.

1705 First 'industrial' suburb of Glasgow built, at Calton, for linen spinners and weavers.

1707 Union between England and Scotland gives Glasgow access to profitable new markets in England and English colonies.

1745 Bonnie Prince Charlie and his Jacobite army come to Glasgow. Glaswegians do not support them.

1762 Ocean-going shipbuilding begins in Glasgow.

1768 Work begins to create a deep-water channel so

that ships can sail up the Clyde to Glasgow.

1769 James Watt patents new steam-engine design.

1776 United States Declaration of Independence ends Glasgow's tobacco trade.

1786 Some of Scotland's first water-powered cotton-spinning mills built at New Lanark, near Glasgow.

1787 Workers at Calton stage Scotland's first industrial strike.

1790–1793 Forth and Clyde and Monkland canals completed; Glasgow now connected to Scottish east coast ports.

1792 First steam-powered cotton-spinning mill in Glasgow.

1797 Charles Tennant invents new process for bleaching cloth; opens chemicals factory.

1800 City of Glasgow Police founded.

c. 1800 Now 114 schools in Glasgow, plus two universities and a medical college.

1800–1830 Iron foundries in Glasgow and along the Clyde.

1802 World's first steam-powered boat, *Charlotte Dundas*, runs on Forth and Clyde canal.

1812 First commercial steam-powered ship, *The Comet*, launched on the Clyde.

1820 Radical War: calls for a general strike and rebellion by workers.

1820s–1850s Glasgow cotton exported worldwide.

1823 First Jewish migrants arrive.

1826–1831 First steam-powered Scottish locomotives made in Glasgow.

1828 Neilson's Hot Blast furnace invented in Glasgow; revolutionises iron production.

1830 Robert Napier designs new steam boilers for ships.

1830–1900 Glasgow expands south across the Clyde (industry and workers' homes), east (industry); and west (residential districts).

1831 Horse-drawn Glasgow and Garnkirk Railway brings coal.

1833 Glasgow Necropolis (grand new cemetery).

1837 Parkhead Forge opens; mass production of iron and steel.

1837 Cotton-spinners strike for shorter working hours.

1840s Peak years of migration by Irish people and Scottish Highlanders to Glasgow.

1840s Production of iron-hulled passenger ships starts in Glasgow.

1840s–1850s 'Railway mania': Glasgow now has rail connections to Scottish towns and to England.

1841–1848 Chartist (democratic reform) campaigns.

1842 Glasgow Botanic Gardens open.

1844 Glasgow Stock Exchange opens.

1859 Queen Victoria opens Glasgow's new water supply.

1861 American Civil War disrupts supplies of raw cotton; Glasgow cotton industry declines.

1862 Glasgow appoints first City Medical Officer.

1865 Joseph Lister pioneers antiseptic surgery.

1865 Singer sewing machine factory opens.

1866 City Improvement Trust starts to clear slums.

1874 Glasgow produces over half the UK's new ships.

1875 Sir William Macewen pioneers new surgery.

1880s Glasgow shipping companies dominate world sea routes.

1893 Glasgow's first electricity power station.

1896 John Macintyre opens world's first X-Ray department.

1888 and 1901 Great Exhibitions at Glasgow.

1896 Glasgow Subway opens.

1898–1902 First electric trams in Glasgow.

1903 North British Locomotive Company exports worldwide.

1906–1914 Glasgow suffragettes protest.

1911 Mass strike at Singer sewing machine factory.

1914–1915 Glasgow women lead rent strike.

1914–1918 Over 200,000 Glasgow men fight in World War I.

1919 'Red Clydeside': Glasgow workers riot.

1919–1938 As city boundaries expand, Glasgow council builds 35,000 new homes for workers.

1920s–1930s Economic depression; Glasgow industry slumps; one-third of workers unemployed.

1930s Glasgow gangland 'wars'.

1938 Glasgow hosts last-ever Empire Exhibition.

1941 Clydebank Blitz – German bombing raids.

1947 New town (Cumbernauld) re-houses Glasgow families.

1953 First high-rise slum clearance flats built.

1960s Motorways built through the centre of Glasgow.

1969 Last great ocean liner built in Glasgow (QE II); Glasgow docks and shipbuilders close.

1970–1980 Glasgow iron, steel and heavy industrial works close.

1983 'Glasgow Smiles Better' campaign.

1983 Burrell Collection opens; world-class art.

1988 Glasgow Garden Festival.

1990 Glasgow is European City of Culture.

2001 New International Financial Services District.

2002 and 2007 Glasgow hosts UEFA football Cup Final.

2011 Glasgow is Scotland's most ethnically diverse city.

2014 'Glasgow City Region' established.

2014 Glasgow hosts Commonwealth Games.

2018 Glasgow hosts European Championships (athletics).

2019 Launch of Glasgow City Innovation District (Scotland's first) to pioneer new developments in business, technology and the creative industries.

2019 Glasgow voted one of the world's Top Ten places to visit.

Index

Some other
Very Peculiar Histories™

The Blitz
David Arscott
ISBN: 978-1-907184-18-5

Kings & Queens
Antony Mason
ISBN: 978-1-906714-77-2

Castles
Jacqueline Morley
ISBN: 978-1-907184-48-2

London
Jim Pipe
ISBN: 978-1-907184-26-0

Charles Dickens
Fiona Macdonald
ISBN: 978-1-908177-15-5

Scotland
Fiona Macdonald

Golf
David Arscott
ISBN: 978-1-907184-75-8

Vol. 1: From ancient times
to Robert the Bruce
ISBN: 978-1-906370-91-6

Great Britons
Ian Graham
ISBN: 978-1-907184-59-8

Vol. 2: From the Stewarts
to modern Scotland
ISBN: 978-1-906714-79-6

Ireland
Jim Pipe
ISBN: 978-1-905638-98-7

Wales
Rupert Matthews
ISBN: 978-1-907184-19-2

Whisky
Fiona Macdonald
ISBN: 978-1-907184-76-5

For the full list, visit
www.salariya.com

Should it stay or should it go?

Since the 1980s, an orange plastic traffic cone has 'adorned' the equestrian statue of the Duke of Wellington (yes, the one who won the battle of Waterloo) that stands in a prominent position in Glasgow's city centre. Completed in 1844, the figure of the Iron Duke makes a proud, dignified statement. And it's surrounded by magnificent Victorian buildings and promenades.

Originally, the cone was perched on top of the Duke's head as a dangerous, if admirably athletic, prank by drunken revellers. It was soon removed by Glasgow Council, but has been replaced – and removed again – countless times. In 2013, because of removal expenses (estimated at £10,000 a year), to prevent damage to a fine work of art, and because climbing the slippery bronze is undoubtedly risky, Glasgow Council planned to raise the statue high out of public reach. An outcry followed, the plans were cancelled and – so far – the cone remains.